The **Rough Guide** to

# Travel Survival

## THE ESSENTIAL FIELD MANUAL

Written and researched by

**Doug Lansky**

# Contents

# Introduction

Travel is delightfully (and frustratingly) unpredictable. If you usually bring a torch or a few tablets of Imodium when you travel, then you're already anticipating that your journey may not go exactly as planned. It rarely does. When a more serious emergency situation arises, how you react can directly determine your life span, and even in a developed country the world's best insurance policy won't do you much good when you need immediate help. This portable, easy-to-follow field manual is designed to bridge that treacherous gap between when you first run into trouble and when you're eventually reimbursed by your insurance provider.

Foreign correspondents, photojournalists and international aid workers aren't the only ones who venture into exotic locales. Adventurous independent travellers, businessmen working on remote projects, and even adventure package tourists are increasingly heading into more isolated regions in that relentless pursuit of the road less travelled. This book is designed to function as a field guide for those who have no experience with survival and serve as a helpful checklist for those who've already taken a survival course but want to make sure they remember everything in a difficult situation.

We're all natural survivalists, hardwired with some basic survival abilities (humans can generally live for about three hours without warmth in extremely cold conditions, about three days without water and about three weeks without food). The problem is our fight-or-flight reaction, which can convert into pure panic without something to fight or run from, making stupid decisions difficult to avoid. There's no such thing as a magic plan for every sort of emergency – there are simply too many variables. But there is a basic strategy, a checklist of sorts that experienced survivalists will run through. Pilots and trauma medics employ a similar approach when faced with crisis situations – they carry a checklist because they know that stress could cause them to think less clearly. The strategies outlined in this book will help you prioritize and think through your situation and greatly increase your odds of making a smart decision.

Statistically, you're most likely to use this guide because you've got lost, lost mobility because of an injury, experienced extreme weather conditions, got caught off guard by nightfall, wandered into an unsafe part of a city, or your vehicle's broken down. Most people stranded in developed nations are found within 24 hours of searching, and nearly all are rescued within three days – but you'll still need to know how to get by until help arrives.

Survival is determined by your mindset, knowledge, experience, supplies, gear, physical conditioning, preparation – and luck. As well as helping you prepare fully, this book offers basic survival information split into specific environments to assist with crucial judgement calls that depend on your situation. Each chapter contains a checklist of what to do in an emergency. The illustrated tips and tricks throughout the book will help you get warm, rested, hydrated and nourished and avoid potential pitfalls as you make your way to safety. But because there's little substitute for actual field experience, we've also included a list of useful courses you can take before you go.

I have spent over ten years on the road in over one hundred countries as an independent traveller and travel columnist. That hardly qualifies me as a survival expert, but I've used this invaluable experience to distil technical information from the world's top experts into travel-specific, reliable and fool-proof techniques and tips – survival for travellers who haven't got time to study it. I hope it helps you stay safe.

## Currency

We've used US dollars throughout this book. At the time of writing the conversion rates were as follows:

| US $1 = | |
|---|---|
| UK | £0.57 |
| | €0.83 |
| | AUS$1.34 |
| | NZ$1.49 |
| | CAN$1.22 |

# Preparation

# Preparation

# Preparation

Although this book comprises tips and strategies for surviving innumerable situations around the world, there's no getting away from the fact that a little pre-trip groundwork can help ensure a safe return. This chapter aims to help you equip yourself with a basic survival kit, some vital travel documents and methods of addressing security issues, so you're well prepared and more confident when venturing off-piste.

When you prepare, it's worth bearing in mind these **rules to live by**:

- Know your limits. If you want to venture into rough areas, consider a course to improve your knowledge, or travel with someone who is trained (such as a guide).
- Plan for worst-case weather and pack accordingly.
- Carry a basic medical and survival kit.
- Inform a trusted friend or family member (plus local officials) when heading into volatile or wilderness areas.
- Stay up to date with local politics so you're not caught off guard by riots, protests or skirmishes.

## Figuring out if a destination is safe to visit

At the time of writing, the US State Department had 26 countries on its "no go" list. Of those countries included, however, there's a serious difference between the safety for a traveller in Nepal and for one in Iraq. Likewise between Israel and Afghanistan or Indonesia and Liberia. Also, India isn't on the list, but you certainly should think twice before hanging out in the Kashmir area. Many countries with long-standing consular warnings have been safely visited by travellers for years; the best way to treat these travel warnings is to use them as a basis for further investigation, including checking if your insurance provider will cover you once you get there. To figure out which countries are really dangerous and which are just perceived as such, even when they are actually safe, cheap, and relatively devoid of tourists, you'll need to do some basic research. Because political conditions change often, make sure you're armed with the latest information before deciding to go, and keep updated while you're on the road.

## Government websites

Get the official position, but keep in mind that a country can be safe but for a single, remote border dispute. The UK Foreign Office website (⊕www.fco .gov.uk) is more likely than the others to specify the volatile area when they place an entire country on warning. You might cross-check with Canada's Consular Affairs Department (⊕www.voyage.gc.ca), Australia's Department of Foreign Affairs (⊕www.dfat.gov.au) or the US State Department (⊕www.travel.state.gov).

## Travel guides

Nearly all the major guidebooks have security information and often go into greater depth on particular (dangerous) regions, which can help explain why travel to certain countries is advised against, even when the destination has been a popular choice with travellers for years. It's useful background knowledge, but even recent editions can be outdated on security by the time they reach the bookshelves, so you'll want to take another step or two.

## Travel advisories

Try World Travel Watch (⊕www.travelerstales.com/wtw) or Lonely Planet's Travel Ticker (⊕www.lonelyplanet.com/travel_ticker). Even these travel-friendly sites tend to be compiled from government reports and news agencies, so you don't hear about the millions who have sidestepped the violence completely, or how isolated it is.

## Tourist bureaus and embassies

You can surf the Web for tourist bureaus and embassies (or try ⊕www.towd .com and ⊕www.escapeartist.com/embassy1/embassy1.htm), where you'll almost always find an email address of a specific office within a country. Tourist bureau staff generally have a good feel for travel conditions in their country; tell them your nationality, when you're planning to travel and roughly where you hope to go, and they'll inform you as to any security issues you should be concerned about. Pose the same question to your embassy in that country. Keep in mind that the tourist bureau may be overly promotional and the embassy staff overly cautious.

## Chat rooms and webpostings

Visit chat rooms and webpostings. You can find out information directly from travellers who've recently been to destinations or are still in the country. Try

Rough Guides' message board, Travel Talk (www.roughguides.atinfopop. com), or Lonely Planet's Thorn Tree (www.thorntree.lonelyplanet.com).

## Learn about local weather conditions

Many of the people who die on mountains set off on day hikes in summer conditions with little more than the T-shirt on their backs, only to find that things can turn nasty on the brightest day. Try to think about all weather eventualities before you travel – find out as much as possible about the weather conditions in your destination (contact park rangers and tourist offices) and take gear and make back-up plans accordingly.

### Dressing for the weather

Your clothing is your first line of defence against the elements and could end up being the only shelter you have. Don't just dress for the environment you're in, dress for the environment you're travelling through or over. Before departing on vehicles that could potentially break down in the middle of nowhere, check weather conditions that may occur. You may wish, for example, to bring along extra warm clothes if heading over a high pass or extra water when passing through a desert.

## Choosing a tour operator

Before you put your life in the hands of a tour operator, do a little research.

- **Check for credentials.** Are the guides qualified to be leading that level of trip, eg, is a trained mountain guide taking you up the mountain or a local guy with a torch and a tent?
- **Look at reviews of other clients.** Try to get email addresses of previous clients from the tour operator and ask them yourself.
- **Check the local tourist office** to see if they've had any complaints about that tour company.

You may also wish to ask the operator a few questions:

- **Has the guide been trained in first aid?**
- **Will the guide be taking an extensive first-aid kit?**
- **What are the guide's credentials and how many times has the guide led this trip?**
- **Are they fully insured?**

## Making your own survival kit

Prepackaged survival kits are widely available, but when you know what to include, it's easy to put together your own personalized kit, which you can then drop into a small, waterproof carrying case. If you're going to the trouble of getting items à la carte, get quality stuff – your life may depend on it.

❑ whistle
❑ mirror
❑ 1–3m duct tape (wrap around a pen or water bottle to save space)
❑ 2–10m wire for snares (easy to bend, holds its shape and is difficult to break with hands)
❑ 3–20m nylon cord/parachute cord
❑ large sewing needle
❑ 1 small spool of fishing line (10kg test strength)
❑ pocket knife with locking blade
❑ fishing hooks (several small sizes only)
❑ sinker weights for fishing
❑ waterproof torch (flashlight)
❑ LED keychain light with constant "on" switch
❑ 2 different types of fire-starting tools (lighter/waterproof matches/flint)
❑ waterproof tinder
❑ space blanket
❑ 1–3 candles
❑ collapsible water-carrying pouch
❑ water-purification tablets
❑ compass
❑ sunblock (at least SPF 25)
❑ safety pins
❑ energy bars
❑ wire saw
❑ 1 sq metre heavy-duty aluminium foil (folded)
❑ 1–2 large plastic rubbish bags
❑ dental floss (for sewing)
❑ surveyor's tape (for marking your path when lost)

### Environment-specific items

**Jungle:** hammock*, plastic tarp*, mosquito net*, mosquito repellent*, machete*
**Desert:** collapsible water containers, plastic tarp*, sand goggles

**Ocean:** reverse osmosis pump* (converts saltwater to drinking water), plastic tarp, flares*

**Mountain/Arctic:** survival bag*, chemical handwarmers*, extra tinder, bear spray*, avalanche equipment (beacon, probe, shovel)

**War zones/dangerous cities:** extra wallet*, white handkerchief*

\* can be easily found in local towns near relevant environment

## Making your own medical kit

Most prepackaged first-aid kits provide supplies for only the most basic emergencies and typically come in nylon sacks that don't keep your bandages and pills from getting wet or crushed. Consider making your own. Start out with a sturdy waterproof container and pay extra attention to environment-specific items (such as more sports tape for hikers, altitude-sickness medicine for mountain climbers or aspirin for those who plan to spend a good deal of time at the bar).

Many travellers feel safer if they carry **antibiotics**; if you're whacking your way through a rainforest for weeks, it's probably a good idea to see a doctor about potential medical problems and prescriptions you may need as a precaution. But in every big city, you're never that far from a local medic or hospital. If you get sick enough to require antibiotics, you should really be visiting a doctor, who can prescribe the best ones for your condition. If you do take antibiotics that you have brought along with you, take the full course as recommended by the doctor, even if your symptoms abate after just one or two days. Otherwise, the few microbes that don't get killed off tend to mutate and come back stronger. The same applies for **syringes**; you won't need them unless you're spending a considerable time in extremely remote areas.

You will also need to talk to your doctor about **malaria prophylactics** which you should begin taking before travelling to affected regions (but note that malaria is often not present in the major gateway cities to the regions, so plan accordingly).

- ❑ elastic wrap bandage
- ❑ anti-diarrhoea medicine
- ❑ laxatives
- ❑ antihistamines
- ❑ hydrocortisone cream (for stings and bites)
- ❑ aspirin/paracetamol
- ❑ iodine/antiseptic

- ❏ re-hydration mix packets
- ❏ plasters (band-aids)
- ❏ blister plasters
- ❏ Tiger Balm (sore muscles, colds, headaches, insect bites)
- ❏ gauze
- ❏ non-lubricated condoms (useful for carrying things in as well as preventing STDs and unwanted pregnancy)
- ❏ tweezers
- ❏ petroleum jelly
- ❏ sports tape
- ❏ motion-sickness pills
- ❏ anti-inflammatory pills (ibuprofen)

## Expedition medicine (prescription required)

As well as the following medicines, those on an expedition should consider bringing a traction device, such as: Hare Traction Splint, Sager Traction Splint or Kendrick Traction Device.

- Cyprofloxacin (urinary tract infection, upset stomach; do not take with anti-inflammatory medication)
- Erythromycin (respiratory infections and campylobacter; do not take with antihistamines)
- Fluxloxacillin (soft-tissue infections)
- Chloramphenicol ointment (eye infections)
- Metronidazole (giardia, dysentery, dental infections; do not take with alcohol)
- Acetazolamide (Diamox; high-altitude sickness prevention and cure for mild cases)
- Dexamethasone (Decadron; severe high-altitude cerebral edema)
- Nifedipine (severe high-altitude pulmonary edema)

# Emergency numbers and documents

- **Add the following phone numbers to the last page of this book:** credit-card and insurance hotlines, your doctor, mobile-phone provider, airlines you're flying with and airline ticket numbers.
- **Make 2 photocopies of the following** (leave one copy with someone you trust, take the other and pack it in a different place from the originals): passport, airline tickets, proof of purchase of airline tickets,

## Electronic gadgets

**Triple-band mobile phones** work in almost all countries (a waterproof cover is a good idea), but the main problem with any mobile is the lack of coverage in remote areas – where you often need help most – and battery life. A **satellite phone** may be better in remoter spots; Iridium (🌐www.iridium .com) provides global satellite coverage, Globalstar (🌐www.globalstar.com) isn't quite global and Thuraya (🌐www.thuraya.com) and ACeS (🌐www .acesinternational.com) are regional. There are, however, a few drawbacks with these too. You need to be outside to use them and even then the signal is easily blocked by nearby trees, high terrain or buildings. Portable units have come down in size in recent years but are still considerably bulkier than mobile phones and cost roughly $1400. Limited battery life is also an issue. Waterproof pouches are available, but it makes them even bulkier still. Search-and-rescue teams can't home in on a satellite phone's signal and (except for Thuraya) they have no internal locating ability.

A handheld **GPS (Global Positioning System)** device taps into a network of 24 satellites to establish your position and the more advanced models can show you where you are on a small digital map. They can also tell you how fast you're going and your direction of travel and can plot the course you've already taken. Many are even waterproof. What they can't do is show you the best way through nature's obstacles (and again the battery supply isn't infinite). A **PLB (Personal Locator Beacon)** transmits a digital signal on an emergency radio frequency which alerts potential rescuers to your presence and helps them locate you. Newer models are smaller than some satellite phones, weigh less and cost around $500. The beacon doesn't let you speak to rescuers, but these devices are waterproof (not submersible) and transmit for at least 24 hours at minus 20°C. Some even have built-in GPS. PLB signals are often picked up from inside boats and buildings (although they cannot pass through rock or thick concrete), but forest canopies and other tall objects can interfere with the signal, so signalling from a clearing is advisable.

While it doesn't hurt to have any of the above gadgets (a PLB is the most foolproof of the bunch), they can lead to a false sense of security. In remote areas of developing countries, there's often not an effective search and rescue response no matter how good your signal. If you carry a phone, satellite phone, beacon or GPS, always make plans as if you didn't have it.

*Written in consultation with **Doug Ritter**, a journalist and survival-equipment consultant who helps test survival gear. His reports have been included in reference collections of the US Air Force Survival School and the US National Search and Rescue School. He runs the website 🌐www.equipped.org.*

Worldwide emergency numbers and emergency citizen services numbers at your embassy are found on pp.202–215; emergency radio frequencies are found on p.194.

credit cards, driver's licence, eye-glass prescription, medical prescriptions, list of inoculations (with dates), insurance policy.

- **Set up an online vault to access this information (such as ⓦwww.ekit .com) or email it to yourself and keep it in your mailbox.**
- **Get about 10 passport photos taken.** For visa applications on the road.
- **Take a list of English-speaking doctors in the places you're visiting.** Join IAMAT (ⓦwww.iamat.org) for a worldwide list.
- **Bring a phone card with local numbers to make international calls.** This is an easy way to reverse the charges or bill the charges to an account. Your national phone carrier will probably provide these services, but there are (usually) cheaper alternatives, such as ⓦwww.ekit.com.

## Keeping others updated

The more information you leave behind you, the better the chances of successful search and rescue should you get lost. Give an itinerary to a trusted friend or family member; they're your best advocates and can push a rescue operation into action if need be. Also leave a copy with rangers at parks or, if you're heading into a volatile or wilderness region not within a park, embassy officials. Include the following information:

- Route plan.
- Emergency routes. Take a look at your route and consider how you may get back to civilization quickly if you should need to do so. Mark this on your route plan.
- Your mobile/satellite phone number.

## Health

- **Get a checkup.** If you're leaving on a long trip, a health and dental checkup prior to departure are advised. It's better to catch small aliments before they become serious in a place where you can't easily get treatment.
- **Get vaccinated.** Start by visiting ⓦwww.cdc.gov/travel. Enter the regions you're planning to visit and the website will spit out which vaccinations you may need. Ring your local travel clinic for a consultation and

appointment (you may wish to ring several to compare prices if you're not covered by your private or national health plan). If the clinic's suggestions differ from the list you got from the CDC, ask why. If their answers sound fishy, get a second opinion.

- **Train for your trip.** Maintaining a moderate or high level of fitness may seem like a bonus at home, but it can actually keep you alive in a situation that requires intense hiking, climbing, treading water or paddling.

## Insurance

Even if insurance can't always help you on the spot, it's invaluable when things go wrong. Good insurance can do more than reimburse lost luggage, plane tickets and medical bills: it can get you air-ambulanced out of a country or have your family brought to you if you're unable to fly. It can also help if you need translation and legal assistance or if you get into trouble with the law. If anything does happen to you and you're not insured, you or your family could face a massive bill. Rescue operations and hospital care can easily run as high as $100,000.

- **Check your medical and homeowner's insurance to see where the coverage leaves off.** You'll almost certainly require many aspects of travel insurance, but try to find a policy that doesn't overlap insurance you're already paying for.
- **Consider what activities you may be doing.** If you're skiing, climbing, trekking or bungy-jumping when you get injured, you may not be covered. Many policies require special supplements for coverage during these (and many other activities). Check the small print – scan the policy for a list of activities (they're usually crammed into one or two paragraphs). If you have any doubts or don't see an activity that you're intending to do, investigate further.
- **Consider where you're going.** Some policies may not cover you if you're heading to a country on an official travel advisory list. Check the policy for this wording or ask.
- **Compare policy prices.** Once you know what you're looking for, you can compare prices. Travel Insurance Center (ⓦwww.worldtravelcenter .com) has excellent comparison features on its website and offers special insurance for war- and terrorism-affected areas. You might compare what you find there with a policy from International SOS (ⓦwww .sosinternational.com), which claims to be the world's largest evacuation

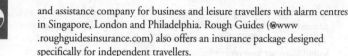

and assistance company for business and leisure travellers with alarm centres in Singapore, London and Philadelphia. Rough Guides (ⓦwww .roughguidesinsurance.com) also offers an insurance package designed specifically for independent travellers.

• **Make sure a member of your family has a copy of your policy.** If you're hospitalized abroad, for example, they should be able to see that they have the right to be flown to visit you. If you have a policy that covers funds in the event of your death, your family needs to be able to collect.

## Taking a survival course

Professional instructors and a challenging terrain can provide things this book can't: hands-on experience and confidence. You wouldn't want to learn how to swim as you're abandoning a sinking ship. If you decide not to take a course, it's worth trying out a few skills before you actually embark on a trip. Locate the North Star, learn to tie a few knots, start a fire in windy conditions, spend the night in your garden in winter with just a sleeping bag, tarp and a candle – anything you've tried at least once before will give you an advantage in a survival situation. There are hundreds of survival courses on offer worldwide; a comprehensive list can be found at ⓦwww.equipped.org. Below are schools run by the experts who've contributed to this book.

**Aboriginal Living Skills School**
Prescott, Arizona, USA
☏928-713-1651
ⓦwww.alssadventures.com
Desert survival, winter camping and primitive camp-craft skills with one-day to week-long courses.

**Adventure Lifesigns**
Aldershot, Hampshire, UK
☏01252 326555
ⓦwww.lifesignsgroup.co.uk
Expedition training, remote medical training and independent travellers' courses. Expedition medical courses run from one to four days.

**Boulder Outdoor Survival School (BOSS)**
Boulder, Colorado, USA

☎303-444-9779
🌐www.boss-inc.com
Wilderness survival courses in a high desert setting in Boulder, Utah, or winter survival in the Rocky Mountains. Courses range from four to 28 days.

## Centurion Risk Assessment Services
Andover, Hants, UK
☎ 01264 355255
🌐www.centurion-riskservices.co.uk
Five-day HEFAT (Hostile Environment and First Aid Training) courses for journalists and international organizations.

## Karamat Wilderness Ways
Edmonton, Alberta, Canada
☎780-325-2345
🌐www.karamat.com
Wilderness survival specializing in the northern boreal forests. Courses run from two to six days.

## LTR (Learn To Return) Training Systems, Inc.
Anchorage, AK, USA
☎907-563-4463
🌐www.survivaltraining.com
Emergency survival training in arctic, mountain and sea environments, as well as for natural disasters, industrial accidents and terrorist attacks. Over 25 specialized courses that range from two to 96 hours.

## Objective Team
Daventry, Northants, UK
☎01788 899 029
🌐www.objectiveteam.com
Specialized corporate training for hostile environments and one-day, gap-year classes in London and around the UK.

## Randall's Adventure & Training
Blaine, Tennessee, USA (courses in Peru)
☎856-932-9111
🌐www.jungletraining.com
Jungle survival instruction with courses ranging from six days with the Peruvian Air Force school to sixteen-day expeditions.

**Wilderness Medical Associates**
Bryant Pond, Maine, USA
☎207-665-2707
ⓦwww.wildmed.com
Wilderness medical and rescue courses ranging from two days to a month-
long EMT plus Wilderness Emergency Medical Training, first aid and
wilderness and rescue medicine.

# Travelling safely

# Travelling safely

# Travelling safely

Whether you're travelling around the world or around your own country, you're likely to be setting foot in new and unfamiliar territory. There's a tendency to relax and enjoy the local pace, but in order to stay safe, you also need to stay alert. Finding that balance is the trick. This chapter covers a few steps that will help you avoid common pitfalls and recover quickly when things go wrong.

## What to do if everything is stolen

Having all of your belongings stolen can be scary and demoralizing but, fortunately, it's not nearly the hassle it used to be. As long as you're prepared and have taken advantage of more recent technology, you could very well have everything you need in one business day. Act immediately to get the process started the moment you realize you've been robbed.

1. **Cancel credit cards and bar mobile phones.** You can locate reverse-charge (collect) call numbers in many guidebooks, the back page of the *International Herald Tribune*, or even ring a local phone operator. If you have already given your travel insurance company all of these details, let them do the calling for you.
2. **Report the incident.** Tell the police what happened and get a numbered copy of the report of the incident.
3. **Get some money wired to you.** If your insurance or credit-card providers aren't sending you emergency cash (or aren't sending much), get some wired to you using Western Union (ⓦwww.westernunion.com) or MoneyGram (ⓦwww.moneygram.com). The transfer typically takes a few minutes and in many countries you can collect up to $999 with a test question that you answer in lieu of ID. If to collect the money you must give ID, and yours is stolen, you could ask for the sum to be transferred to a travelling companion who can supply their own ID.
4. **Call your nearest embassy, consulate or high commission.** Tell them what has happened. They'll want to know your departure date and may request that, if possible, you wait a few days to see if your passport turns up. Don't expect food and lodging from them, but it is to be hoped they'll be sympathetic and do their best to speed the process along.

5.  **Gather what you need for your passport replacement:**
    *   **A police report.**
    *   **Copies of your documents (see p.14).** The most important of these is a copy of your passport's photo page. A copy of your driver's licence or any other formal ID is helpful.
    *   **Photos.** Check with the embassy for photo requirements before getting your photos taken.
    *   **Replacement forms.** If you have access to the Web, you can often print out and complete the lost/stolen passport forms from your embassy's website before you arrive.
    *   **Fee.** This differs from country to country and can depend on whether you're getting a permanent replacement or temporary emergency passport and how quickly you need it. The embassy will inform you when you call, but expect to pay roughly $50–100.
6.  **If you have no copies of your documents or access to any cash, throw yourself on the mercy of your embassy.** If you're travelling with another citizen from your country with a valid passport, have them come along and vouch for you. Have your friends or parents fax any documents they have (old photo ID, pictures, birth certificate, etc) directly to the embassy.

## Replacing airline tickets

Some airlines may ask you to buy a completely new ticket, but will then reimburse you once the lost ticket is past its validity date (to ensure it's not used by someone else).

*   **Contact the airline's airport counter or one of the local airline offices for advice.** Getting a replacement ticket will be easier if you have proof of purchase, a photocopy of the ticket or the original ticket number. Take along a copy of the police report plus any documentation from your embassy showing your replacement of documents (a newly reissued passport would be good). You may need to pay an administrative fee (about $50 per ticket).
*   **For charter tickets contact the tour operator's representative.** Replacing these should be more straightforward. Your name should suffice if you can demonstrate (with a newly reissued passport or police report) that you've had everything stolen. You may, however, still incur a fee (typically about $30), depending on the company.

# Thwarting pickpockets and thieves

Travellers are prime targets of theft. They're distracted by sights, carry an abundance of money, and are unlikely to stick around long enough to testify in court. There are a few simple things you can do, however, to make yourself less of a target.

- **Get everything into one bag – the smaller the better.** Take one piece of luggage, preferably a backpack. Packing light not only shows that you don't have much to steal, it also allows you to keep one or both hands free and helps you remain mobile, so robbing you appears more difficult.

- **Keep valuables hidden.** Remove all jewellery and cover rings with a band-aid or tape (unless you specifically want to demonstrate that you're married). If you wear a watch make sure it's cheap and looks it. Don't store your camera in a case marked with a camera brand name and be particularly alert when you're using it.

- **Use a fake wallet.** Keep your cards and documents in a passport pouch under your clothing, but keep your pocket change in a thin wallet with a photo, some outdated cards, and $5–20. If a pickpocket or mugger does get it, he won't get much.

- **Blend in.** Plan to pick up some clothes when you arrive; look for the Western-style clothes that the locals are wearing (not a traditional outfit, which may make you stand out more). The simpler the outfit the better, and dark colours are preferable.

- **Avoid dangerous areas.** Ask someone at your hotel or in the tourist information office to mark the dangerous areas of town on your map (for both day and night). If you inadvertently wander into an area that feels risky or you think you're being followed, duck into a police station or a reputable-looking shop or hop into a taxi. For just a small amount of cash, you can quickly get back to a safer area a few blocks away.

- **Disguise your pack.** Padlocks and wire-mesh pack covers are not as effective as you may think and will draw attention to the value of your

▲ Backpack in a rice sack

bag's contents. Burlap sacks and plastic rice bags are cheap and easy to find and make great pack covers. Cut four slits for your shoulder straps, disconnect them, feed them through, then reconnect.

- **Don't drop your guard.** Get into the habit of checking over your shoulder and across the street every now and then.

## Foiling a scam artist

Most scams are variations on a number of themes, and when you are able to recognize these you will be better equipped to spot the con artist from the many genuinely kind people out there. Listed below are a few of the classics.

### Border crossing scam

You become an unknowing drug mule when a seemingly innocent person asks you for the small favour of helping deliver a package, carry a suitcase, or push a pushchair (stroller) across a border.

**How to avoid:** Never, never, never carry anything over a border for anyone, even if it's just a postage stamp for a nun in a wheelchair. You should also keep an eye on your luggage. Padlocks may not keep thieves from getting into your luggage, but they do help keep smugglers from putting things in.

### Drug buy scam

You buy a small amount of drugs from a local dealer who tips off his buddy, the police officer. The police officer then comes knocking at your door to demand a fee for not taking you to prison.

**How to avoid:** It's a dangerous game of chicken. You can pay the fine, try to bargain a little, or call their bluff and tell them you have no money, you were set up and that you're happy to go to police headquarters and explain it. However, it's best just to avoid buying the drugs in the first place.

### Credit card scam

A store owner takes your credit card to a back room to swipe it, then swipes it again for another price. You sign one, then he forges your signature on the other.

**How to avoid:** Keep a close eye on your credit card and ask the person to run it through the machine in front of you. Hold onto the receipt when you make any purchase as a record for your credit-card company.

## Fake police scam

A kid comes up and asks for change for a small note (bill). Not long after, a man approaches, flashes a badge quickly and tells you he's a police officer. He explains that the note you just received is counterfeit and that he needs to take it back to headquarters and you will be fined for your involvement. At this point, just as you are starting to wonder if it's real, a large muscular "colleague" arrives and pressures you to pay up.

**How to avoid:** Take a good long look at his badge and tell the policeman that, although he is certainly a genuine officer, there are many impersonators and that, according to the country's own tourist ministry, you're supposed to make all such spot payment at police headquarters, and you'll be happy to follow him there on foot. Under no circumstances should you get into an "unmarked police car".

## Taxi dash scam

You've paid your taxi and the driver leaves before you can get your bag out of the boot (trunk).

**How to avoid:** Leave your door open or don't pay up until you've got your bag. If there's two of you, one can stay in the taxi until the bags are removed.

## Distraction scam

Someone "accidentally" spills something on you, offers to help you clean it off and robs you in the process. A variation on this is small children thrusting cardboard or newspapers in front of you while their mates pick your pockets.

**How to avoid:** Keep a firm grasp on your belongings, politely refuse any help, and walk off immediately.

## Exchange scam

You get a good price on moneychanging from an unofficial street dealer. He counts out the money with painstaking slowness and finds – in a show of false honesty – that it comes up a few notes short. So he adds a few new notes on top. However, while he's adding the new notes, he's discreetly pulling off even more from the bottom. Before you have a chance to double-check (not that you would, as you've just watched the world's slowest count), he's off.

**How to avoid:** Don't use unofficial moneychangers. If you feel you have to use one, get a recommendation from another traveller and/or make the transaction in a shop or hotel. Have the person put the money in your hand as they count it and always re-count (even at official exchange booths).

### Random acts of kindness

A passerby asks you if you have change for a large note, asks for directions or offers to hold your bag for you. Once you've handed them your bag or opened your wallet, your valuables are as good as gone.

**How to avoid:** When you ask for assistance, chances are you're going to find some lovely, helpful people. When you get approached, you need to be somewhat suspicious.

### Pay it later scam

Your taxi driver tells you not to worry about the price, or the meter, that you'll work it out later. Then, upon reaching your destination, he stings you for many times the actual fare.

**How to avoid:** Ask a local the going rate for a particular journey before you find a cab so you know roughly what it should cost. Always agree on a price before getting into the taxi, or make sure the meter is on. If it's too late, do your best to bargain, try to attract the attention of a nearby police officer and take down the driver's ID number and name so you can report him. Unofficial local tour guides have been known to practise this technique as well.

### Gem scam

A merchant gives you a "great deal" on some uncut gems that he tells you can be resold back home for several times the price. He even offers to throw in the postage and help you mail them. You watch him mail the parcel at the post office but the gems never make it to you back home, or they arrive but turn out to be worthless glass.

**How to avoid:** There are great gem deals, but knowing how to find them takes a professional eye and knowledge of world markets. Don't get involved unless you know exactly what you're doing. If you decide to mail gems, do it yourself, and don't be surprised if customs officials extract a fee on the way into your country before allowing you to claim them.

## For women: avoiding harassment

- **Dress conservatively.** Even if your attire is not racy by your own standards, it might send out the wrong signals. Shorts, short skirts, tank tops, and tight-fitting clothes are likely to denote you as promiscuous in certain parts of the world. Cover your legs and shoulders and keep the clothing baggy.

- **Avoid direct eye contact.**
- **Wear a wedding ring.** Preferably a simple, cheap-looking one. If you're alone, you'll need a story to go with it – something about your husband and children coming to meet you in a day or two.
- **Consider a subtle hairstyle.** A short cut and dark colour draw less attention to yourself. A simple hat is a good way of hiding your hair.
- **Address or forget remarks.** Simply ignore rude remarks, cat calls and pinches and keep walking or react with clarity and confidence (think drill sergeant) and tell them you don't like it.
- **If you get followed, head into a nearby busy shop or police station and tell the owner.**
- **Don't sit at the back of the bus or train.** Pick a seat near other women or a family.
- **Make sure you wear shoes that allow you to run.**

## Surviving a mugging/ attack

- **Be cooperative.** Don't assume they aren't armed just because you can't see a weapon. Your life is worth more than anything you may have in your pocket; you might, however, ask to keep your driver's licence or other "worthless" cards.
- **Be generous.** Try to find a little extra money or trinkets that an attacker may have overlooked; this cooperation could help prevent things getting violent.
- **Run.** Most thieves will

▲ If you feel at all unsafe, stay alert and walk on the outer edge of the pavement (sidewalk), giving you a greater field of vision.

leave satisfied if you give them what they want, but if you believe violence is inevitable, the first step is to get away. You might distract your attacker first by "accidentally" dropping one of the things you're handing over. If he's already got your valuables (or most of them), there's even less chance he'll pursue. Yell for help as you make your getaway.

- **Do not go on the attack.** This is not the time to try out that double-reverse flying back kick you once saw in an Ang Lee movie. Only fight back when physically attacked and go for "low blows": eyes, throat and groin. Use any objects nearby to aid you (a rock, camera or pen, for example).

## Hitchhiking safety tips

1. **Hitch at petrol stations near major motorways.** This allows you to check out potential lifts and approach only those that you would feel comfortable travelling with (the best bet for women hitching alone is a family). Drivers are also more likely to comply when asked directly while they're getting petrol. Hitching at a station also means you can use the facilities while you wait, but you may have to take a local bus to get there initially.

2. **Don't just hop in a car because it pulls over.** Speak to the driver through the window (or open the passenger-side door) and ask them where they're going. Use these few moments to see if the person looks sober and safe; check for open alcohol containers or alcohol on the driver's breath. If you are unsure at all, simply say you're headed elsewhere.

3. **Keep your guard up while in the car.** Don't go to sleep. If you sense that the driver may be drunk, over-fatigued, dangerous or is driving too aggressively, ask them to let you out at the next petrol station. If there aren't any around, have him drop you at a junction (where cars are more likely to slow down), or just get out as soon as possible.

4. **Be ready to act.** If the driver turns off the main road and starts heading in a new direction without telling you, ask to get out of the car immediately. Make it sound casual – if you spot a supermarket or petrol station, point to it and say you need to use the toilet urgently. If you feel your life is in danger and he won't stop to let you out, try hopping out at a junction when the car stops or slows down.

5. **Avoid city centres if passing through.** Don't have a driver drop you in the middle of a city that's not your final destination – hitching out of a

city centre is nearly impossible. It's better to be let off at a petrol station on the motorway just before the city; that way you can catch a ride straight through.

## Making your bus ride safer

Riding buses in developing countries can be one of the most dangerous (and uncomfortable) activities on an independent trip. If the bus is in a really bad condition – the tyres are completely bald for example – opt for a more upmarket option if possible. If there's really no choice, consider the following:

- **Sit near the front.** But not in the front. You get a view of where you're going, can get off in a hurry, have less potential for motion sickness on a curvy road, and still have a few rows in front of you to cushion any collision.
- **Avoid the sun.** Not a lifesaver, but a good idea. Before boarding, figure out which way the bus is headed and which side the sun will be hitting it on. Most buses are not equipped with curtains; direct sunlight means an uncomfortable ride in the stifling air.
- **Go for a window seat.** Assuming it opens, you can control the temperature, get fresh air when feeling nauseous and purchase snacks at bus stops without leaving the bus.
- **Keep an eye on your luggage when the bus stops.** If your luggage is stored underneath or on the roof, watch through the window or get off the bus to get a clear view (a good opportunity to stretch your legs as well).

## Accommodation safety

- **Consider the room location.** In case of fire, it's worth taking into account that the highest fire ladders won't reach past the seventh floor and that fire engines can access only street-side rooms. Avoid the ground and top floors which are the easiest targets for burglars. In areas prone to earthquakes, don't stay above the third floor.
- **Think about fire safety.** Familiarize yourself with the emergency exits and check if there's a smoke detector.
- **Keep your valuables safe.** If you're staying in a dorm, wear your passport pouch at night or store it in your pillowcase; take it with you to the shower if the room is not en suite. Store any other valuables in a locker, both at night and during the day.

### Escaping a hotel fire

1. **Treat all alarms as if they are real.** Never assume it's a drill.
2. **Try to find out where the fire is.** If reception is not answering, try calling an emergency number (see pp.202–215) and ask to be connected to any firemen on the scene.
3. **Check the doorknob for heat.** If there's smoke and fire in the hallway, seal the door with wet towels. If the hallway is clear and you know where the fire is and how to avoid it, go to step 5.
4. **Protect your room while you signal for help.** Soak a bed sheet in water and hang it around your window. Then open the window and yell for help. Throw out a partially unfurled roll of toilet paper, dump some paper, or wave a towel to attract attention.
5. **Escape.** If using emergency routes, take one wet piece of cloth to cover your nose and mouth and another larger one to put over your head. Replace any synthetic-fibre clothing with cotton or, even better, wool, and jump in the shower to wet it down. Always use the stairs, not the lift (elevator). If the door you need to escape through is hot, stand well to the side when opening it because the sudden rush of oxygen will cause any flames to surge. Wait for this surge to pass before fleeing.
6. **Crawl and keep low.** Don't underestimate the danger of smoke inhalation.
7. **Try an alternative escape.** If you can't get rescued and the hallway or emergency exits are blocked, as a last resort, try climbing to another balcony or making a rope from bedsheets to get down. Tie them together with a sheet knot (see p.188).

## Increasing your chances of surviving a plane crash

The National Transportation Safety Board, a US government agency, notes that in plane crashes with fatalities, approximately 32 percent of the passengers survive. The survival rate on flights when the pilot is in control but has to carry out an emergency crash landing goes up to 60 percent. Does it matter which airline? If you're on one of the top 25 safest airlines, chances are 1 in 4.25 million of dying in a plane crash. Flying with the bottom 25 airlines, your chances drop to 1 in 386,000. Is flying safer than driving? Not always. If you compare 100,000 hours of flying time to 100,000 hours of driving time, it's four times safer to take a commercial flight than drive, but twelve times safer to drive than fly a non-scheduled commuter plane (air taxi on demand) and 26 times safer to drive than fly in a private plane.

## Safety precautions

1. **Locate the emergency exits.** Estimate the distance to each one, even count the number of rows between you and those exits. If you can see the exit doors, consider how you would open them.
2. **Make sure your seatbelt is secure and your seat is upright.**
3. **Take a second look at your seatbelt.** Make a mental note about which way it opens and how you could do it with your eyes closed.

## If the plane is crashing

1. **Cushion yourself.** Put a pillow on the lap of small children and have them hold their head against it. Holding a pillow or blanket, brace yourself against the seat in front of you in case the seats accordion together.
2. **Calm yourself.** Try to take deep breaths and remain focused on what you will do after the landing (see below).
3. **Evacuate yourself, not your belongings**. If the cabin is smoky, stay low. Follow the floor safety lights to the red lights marking an exit.

# What to do after a plane crashes

1. **Put distance between you and the plane.** Evacuate 100m upwind of the crash. Planes try to land into the wind, so head in the general direction the plane was taking. Alternatively, look at tree tops and long grass for wind direction.
2. **Provide medical care to those in need.** Ascertain whether any of the survivors has medical training.
3. **Deal with fatalities.** Place them in a row (under a layer of snow if available, otherwise in plastic or dirt). Keep all their personal belongings beside them.
4. **Get organized.** Compile a list of names, ages, injuries and fitness levels of survivors. Add to this what skills people have that may help the situation. Decide on rotating teams, if necessary, to handle the tasks required. Write everything down.
5. **Check the aircraft for usable items.** If the plane seems safe to return to, look for radios, beacons and batteries (which need to be kept warm). The

life raft can be used as a bed or shelter and will contain survival items. Any parachutes or other wind blocks can be used for shelter. Gather any water supplies and anything that can be used to store water. In-flight magazines and can be burned for heat. Duty-free alcohol can be used to help start fires and sterilize wounds.

6. **Collect all in-flight food and centralize it for fair distribution.** Also centralize all matches, lighters and cigarettes and ensure that no flames are inadvertently lit too close to the plane wreckage.

7. **Salvage jet fuel.** Engine parts will remain hot long after a crash, so do not try to salvage immediately. If fuel is dripping or running from the plane, it can be collected in a metal container. Care should be taken with any lighters or matches anywhere near the wreckage. See p.82 for making a fuel fire.

*Written in consultation with **Charlie McGrath**, founder of Objective Travel Safety, who has served fifteen years as a British Army officer in Northern Ireland, Australia, Central America and Southern Africa. He has travelled extensively and now trains war correspondents, NGOs and business professionals in the art of safe travel. Objective Travel Safety also runs a one-day travel safety course in London for gap-year travellers (Ⓦ www.objectivegapyear.com).*

# Arctic and mountain survival

# Arctic and mountain survival

# Arctic and mountain survival

Just because Eskimos aren't whizzing by on dogsleds, and you're not climbing ice walls with crampons and oxygen, doesn't mean you're not at risk from arctic conditions. Technically an "arctic" area is a region where the mean temperature of the warmest month isn't higher than 10°C; there's total darkness or just a few hours of daylight in the winter, and swarms of insects and melting snow that turns tundra into bog in the summer. But the survival information in this chapter will also apply to travellers in less extreme conditions. Many incidents occur on day-hikes up mountains when people head out with little more than a T-shirt and wind jacket. An unexpected storm makes it easy to lose the trail, and an injury as simple as a twisted ankle can create serious problems even for experienced hikers.

If nothing else, make sure you bear in mind these basic **rules to live by** in the arctic:

- Keep clothing dry.
- Shelter yourself with thick insulation.
- Move to keep warm.
- Keep hydrated.
- Build a fire if you can.

## Perceived temperature

| | Temperature °C | | | | | | | |
|---|---|---|---|---|---|---|---|---|
| | 4 | -1 | -7 | -12 | -18 | -23 | -29 | -34 |
| 8kph (2m/s, 5mph) | 2 | -4 | -9 | -15 | -21 | -26 | -32 | -37 |
| 16kph (4m/s, 10mph) | -1 | -9 | -15 | -23 | -29 | **-37** | **-43** | **-51** |
| 32kph (9m/s, 20mph) | -7 | -15 | -23 | **-32** | **-37** | **-46** | **-54** | -62 |
| 48kph (13m/s, 30mph) | -12 | -18 | -29 | **-34** | **-46** | **-54** | -62 | -71 |

Windspeed (left side label)

**Temperatures at which skin may freeze within 1min.**
Temperatures at which skin may freeze within 30 seconds.

# In an arctic or mountain emergency

1. **Get yourself and any companions out of harm's way.**
2. **Address any acute medical problems.** See the medical appendix on pp.171–186.
3. **Take a deep breath and get your bearings.** Don't underestimate the importance of conquering fear and anxiety. See p.186 to help establish your survival mindset.
4. **Shelter.** Exposure is likely to be your greatest immediate threat in this climate. Make sure you're out of the wind as you plan and assess. Windspeed can reduce apparent temperatures by over 100 percent. The colder it is, the more important you get shelter. See p.40 for building specific shelters.
5. **Keep hydrated.** Your need for water is as vital in a cold environment as it is in a warm one. Your sweat may be less noticeable because it gets immediately absorbed into your clothing. See p.43 for ways to get water and p.89 for dehydration signs, prevention and cure.
6. **Plan.** Now that you've dealt with the most pressing issues, read through this entire chapter and cross-referenced sections to prepare more thoroughly for survival. Decide whether you will wait to be rescued or if it will be beneficial to attempt to leave your immediate environment. If in doubt, stay put. Another option for a group is to send one or two pairs of fit volunteers in search of help (in different directions) while the rest of the group remains in place.
   **Reasons to stay put**
   - People are likely to be looking for you.
   - The vehicle you were travelling in or your immediate terrain means that you will be easily spotted from the air.
   - The terrain, weather or injuries will hinder movement. Consider that you may wander into a crevasse, over a cliff or into a high-risk avalanche area. In the summer, boggy tundra can be extremely difficult to cross.
   - The visibility is poor.

# Basic needs

## Maintaining your body temperature

With the best arctic clothing, you can keep your core temperature above freezing, but to survive in cold climates without heated shelter you need to work to make the most of your clothing and warm yourself with activity when necessary.

- You don't have a map/GPS equipment and can't work out the way to civilization.
- The sun will soon set.

**If you stay put**
- Set up a signal (see p.194).
- Scavenge for supplies. Gathering wood and digging snow will keep you active and warm until you need to rest.
- Improve shelter to increase chances of prolonged sleep.
- Once camp is set up, conserve energy by staying very still while you wait for rescuers to spot your signals.

**Reasons to move**
- The terrain you are in is dangerous (due to avalanche, rock slides, animals, etc) or is exposed to the elements.
- You have navigation equipment, necessary gear to handle the terrain, and can determine a realistic route to safety.
- It is unlikely that anyone is looking for you.

**If you move**
- Check around to see if there is anything you can take with you that might aid in survival.
- Leave a clue about which direction you're heading in – logs or rocks forming an arrow – in case anyone shows up. As you progress, leave a trail that could be followed; piles of rocks, for example.
- Put something shiny on your pack or hat (such as a CD or aluminium foil) to attract attention of search crews.
- Don't waste time foraging for food (it's not initially important), but do keep an eye out for known, convenient food sources as you go. See p.44 for food gathering.
- Leave ample time to set up camp each night. Building a shelter can take 30min to 4hr. The days are short and the sun can also drop behind a mountain well before it sets.
- Keep a fire going at night when you stop (search crews may search at night with night-vision goggles).

- **Cover yourself intelligently.** Make sure you keep your head and neck, wrists and hands, and ankles and feet covered. You don't want clothing that's too tight, restricting circulation and limiting the amount of insulating air trapped between layers – adding some hay, dry grass, or crumpled-up newspaper between layers is a good idea, especially at night.
- **Avoid sweating.** While active and warm, uncovering your head and hands is particularly effective heat regulation. Removing clothing when you feel yourself sweating will also keep your clothing dry. With limited

clothing, remove a middle layer garment when you start to sweat and it will provide something dry to put next to your skin once you can relax. Take the opportunity to dry any damp clothing the moment weather permits – hang it up inside your tent overnight.

- **Stay clean.** Washing, though uncomfortable in cold weather, is necessary to avoid rashes and sores. Let your underclothing air out for an hour or two if you're unable to wash it. Clean clothing – with the material free of dirt and oils – breathes best and works most effectively to keep you warm and dry.
- **Let shivering work for you.** Shivering works to keep your body warm so don't fight it when you feel the shivers begin. However, over longer periods, like any activity, it uses up energy and causes fatigue, which leads to a drop in body temperature. Shivering should be a signal to use increased activity to warm up, make shelter or find better insulation for your clothing.
- **Deal with parts at risk.** The biggest frostbite risks are your face, hands and feet. See p.65 for how to avoid and treat frostbite.

## Fire

Getting a fire started quickly is vital; however, one of the most common causes of accidental death in arctic conditions is by fire, so make sure you keep a safe distance and keep flammable materials away. See p.198 for fire starting.

## Shelter

- **Keep it easy.** The shelters below are ordered in terms of how easily they can be made. Deciding which to make will depend on the conditions available, the time you have to create the shelter and the equipment that you have. Always look around for natural shelters or partial shelters to minimize your work (a cave, a trough under a fallen tree or a snowdrift beside a large boulder, for instance). If you need to dig, you can use a cooking pan, snowshoe or any other tools to help.
- **Pace yourself.** Leave plenty of daylight hours to make shelter. Make slow, deliberate movements so you don't break a sweat and get your clothing wet just before you need to sleep.
- **Don't make it too big.** The smaller it is, the less effort it is to make and to keep warm.
- **Put your entrance on the crosswind side.** This keeps the wind out,

and also keeps the snow from blocking the door when it collects on the downwind side.

- **Insulate it.** Don't sleep directly on the ground. Layer the floor with grass, pine needles or extra gear.
- **Ventilate it.** Put a 2-centimetre-diameter hole in a low part of the roof (the highest part of the roof lets too much of the heat out) that you can keep clear with a stick. Block the entrance with a piece of ice or your pack to prevent heat loss.
- **Before sleeping:**
  - **Mark it.** Mark your entrance with a big "X" before entering in case a search plane flies over.
  - **Urinate.** If you need to get up during the night, you'll lose sleep and valuable body heat leaving the shelter. Pee in a bottle or on a pre-cut block of snow that you can throw out of the cave's door.
  - **Remove wet clothes.** Let them freeze, then crush them and shake off the ice. Also remember to brush off any snow on clothing before it melts.
  - **Keep your boots warm.** If you had a fire going, place the small hot stones or hot sand in your wet boots to help dry them and keep warm while you sleep.
  - **Keep your gear with you.** Keep any digging tools inside in case you need to dig your way out. Don't risk any items getting buried or blown away.
  - **Put inhibitions aside.** If you're sharing a snow cave, huddle together. Place elderly people and children in the middle.

## Tree pit

The tree pit is the easiest and quickest shelter since nature has already done most of the work, but it doesn't trap body warmth as well as a snow trench or snow cave. When making a fire, keep some distance from the tree trunk and overhanging branches.

**Time:** 15–30min.

**Gear:** Digging tool and plastic sheet helpful.

- Locate a fir tree with no snow under it, but a wall of snow around the edges.
- Dig on the upwind side of the snow pit. Break off branches from the opposite side of the tree for additional protection and bedding insulation.
- Cover up. Use a plastic sheet or your pack to help with wind protection.

## Snow trench

If there are no trees or sheltered areas and the snow is relatively easy to dig, this option works well for either a single person or a large group. It's quick and easy but not as effective as a good snow cave.

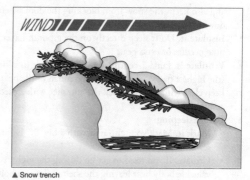

▲ Snow trench

**Time:** 20min–1hr.

**Gear:** Digging tool, wood-cutting tool and plastic sheet helpful.

- **Dig a trench.** It should be at least 50cm deep and 2m wide.
- **Insulate.** Place grass, leaves or twigs on the bottom, if available, to provide insulation between you and the snow.
- **Add height to the upwind end.** Use the dug-out snow, your backpack, a piece of wood or chunk of ice to add height. This can also serve as a door if you have a plastic cover.
- **Roof it.** Pull a plastic tarp over the top of the trench. Or use branches with a layer of snow on top.

## Snow cave

This ideally requires a large snow drift with firm but easy-to-dig snow, but it does provide the most effective shelter.

**Time:** 40min–1hr 30min.

**Gear:** Digging tool, wood-cutting tool and plastic sheet helpful.

- **Find a snowdrift on a slope.**
- **Pick an entrance.** Angle the opening so the wind blows across the opening, not into it or away from it.

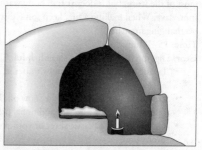

▲ Snow cave, side view

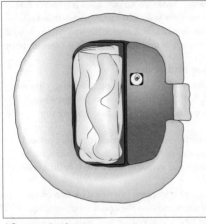
▲ Snow cave, top view

- **Dig straight into the slope and then dig slightly upward.** Make the cave big enough to lie down in and sit up in.
- **Keep it safe.** Don't make it so deep that, should the roof collapse, you will have difficulty digging yourself out.
- **Warm it.** A snow cave will become somewhat warm from your exhaled air and body heat, but you can also use a candle or small cooking stove on low heat (but not a fire) to warm the shelter. Avoid too much condensation, by not boiling more water than necessary. Extinguish any flame before sleeping to avoid carbon monoxide poisoning.
- **Keep the air fresh.** Put a vent hole in the roof.

## Making a hot bed

This is possible only if you have a good fire going.

**Time:** 10–20min.

**Gear:** Grapefruit-sized stones, sticks to carry hot stones.

- **Place stones around fire.** Get them as close as possible.
- **Place branches in the form of a bed.** Or use supple sticks or pine needles on top of any snow or ground.
- **Place the hot rocks on top of the bedding.**
- **Cover the rocks.** Place additional bedding on top of the hot rocks, making sure all the rocks are well covered.

## Water

Water sources in cold regions are generally more sanitary than elsewhere on the planet, especially those found high up mountains. Running water is always preferable to stagnant water; brownish surface water is typically fine after filtration. Ice provides more water and melts more quickly than an equivalent amount of snow. On the coast, blue sea ice has little salt in it, while grey or opaque sea ice contains much more salt and is not fit for consumption.

### Producing water from ice and snow

- **Eat snow only when you're warm.** While moving, travelling, climbing and maintaining high metabolic output, eat snow as you go; when trapped, cold and hungry, you'll lose more heat than gaining any hydration benefit.

- **Using fire.** Place snow or ice in your water bottle (or an old can) and put it close to a fire. Ice can also be melted on a flat rock over a fire and collected in a container. Snow will evaporate and leave very little water; dense snowpack is preferable.

- **Using direct sunlight.** Place your sleeping mat or a dark tarp on an incline and put a chunk of ice or snow on the uphill side. Angle the downhill side of the mat or tarp into a V-shape and place a cup under the edge to catch the melting runoff as the sun warms the ice.

- **Using body heat.** If you're relatively warm, you can melt snow with your body heat by placing it in a plastic bag or bottle and putting it between layers of your clothing. You'll need some water to start out with, however. In the bag or bottle, start with two-thirds water and a third snow. Once melted, drink a third of the contents and add more snow. If you don't have water to begin with, you can use urine as a last resort. After the fourth time adding snow, the urine taste will be lost.

## Finding food

Catching animals is a relatively difficult way to get your nutrition, especially while on the move. Insects and edible plants you can confidently recognize will be a better bet.

### Insects

For information on catching and eating insects, see p.98.

### Plants

Never eat what you don't know or haven't tested properly (see p.197). The following can be found in cold environments: cranberry, blueberry, cloudberry (looks like a yellow raspberry), bilberry, crowberry, salmonberry, spadderdock, Eskimo potato, dandelion and lichens.

### Fishing and trapping

Fishing on frozen waters without a tool to cut through the ice is very difficult, and it's unsafe to stand near a naturally open hole in the ice. See p.130 for fishing techniques. If you see animal tracks you could set a simple trap (see p.190).

# Travel

## Navigating in the arctic

- **The clear arctic air makes estimating distance difficult.** Don't be surprised if the distant landmarks are about three times further away than they appear.
- **Avoid moving in whiteout conditions unless absolutely necessary.** Cirrus clouds (high clouds that look like streaks or curls) coming from a northerly direction that begin to multiply with increased winds indicate a blizzard may be on the way.
- **If close to the poles, a compass can become inaccurate.** Double-check your readings with star (see p.193), stick-and-shadow (see p.192) or wristwatch (see p.191) navigation.
- **Flat terrain can be dangerous.** What look like open fields can in fact be frozen water with melted spots. See p.59 for more on ice safety.
- **Follow a river downstream and it should lead you to civilization.** However, in truly remote areas, distances can be too great. In flat areas with winding rivers, building a raft (see p.108) can speed travel. In mountainous areas, white water can make river travel treacherous.

## Making glasses to avoid sun and snow blindness

Make sure you wear sunglasses if you have them. If you don't, making a pair is quick and easy. You can use any of the following for this, but the material will need to be long enough to wrap around your head: film, paper, cardboard or tree bark. You can always try tucking the ends or edges under a hat if it's too short to secure behind your head. If you have no materials to hand, darken the area beneath your eyes with make-up, shoe polish, soot or charcoal. Be aware that snow blindness can occur during hazy conditions – always take precautions. See p.66 for information on treating sun and snow blindness.

## Making snowshoes

If you are encountering snow that is more than 30cm deep, snowshoes will help movement and keep your feet dryer and warmer. Take your time and make them well to prevent having to fix them while on the move. Check your snowshoes daily and reinforce with extra string and replace any broken sticks.

**Time:** 20–40min per snowshoe.

**Gear:**

- 10 branches – straight, freshly cut, each about three times the length of your foot and about the thickness of your thumb. If you can, substitute hard plastic or metal for any of these; doing so will increase the strength of the snowshoe.
- 10 branches – same as above, except about 15cm long.
- About 1m of string per snowshoe (vine, sapling, wire, canvas strips or leather can also be used).
- Knife.

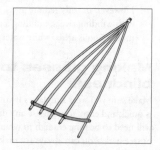

**Directions:**

1. **Tie five branches together at one end with string or wire.** That's the front.
2. **Secure the back of the branches to a shorter branch, leaving a width of two fingers between each one.**
3. **Find the middle of the snowshoe by balancing it on your hand.** On either side of that middle line, secure short branches across, two where the ball of your foot will go and two for the heel.
4. **Bend up the tip several centimetres and use a string to attach it to the front cross section, where the ball of your foot will go.**
5. **Make second snowshoe.**
6. **Place feet on snowshoes and secure with string binding.**

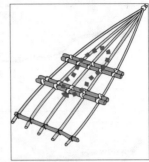

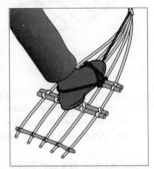

## Picking a survival walking stick

A good walking stick can be used to test ice thickness, pull you out of the ice if you fall through, adjust a campfire, place food in and remove food from the fire, serve as support for a shelter and function as a spear when affixed with a knife.

- **Select a branch from a live or recently fallen tree.** Greener wood won't burn as easily and is less likely to break.
- **Cut a section with the circumference just slightly greater than a table-tennis ball.**
- **Make the stick about head height.**

## Making a sled for pulling gear

If you have ample gear and supplies, carrying it can prove difficult. On snow and ice, a sled will reduce your energy output.

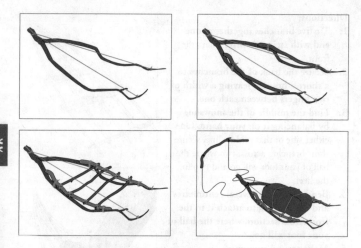

- **An inflatable life raft can be pulled along with gear as a sled and can be used as immediate shelter and an insulated place to rest.**
- **Find one or two branches you can fasten to your waist that will hold your gear.** Make sure you add padding to your waist to avoid chafing.

## Walking over ice

In general, 5cm of ice will support an adult's weight, but 10cm is a safer prospect. Rivers and water with current are less predictable and often more likely to be weaker in spots.

- **Adjust your pack.** Seal a set of dry clothes (along with some trapped air) in two plastic bags and place them in the bottom part of your pack where they will act as extra flotation. Make sure your pack is tight enough not to ride up on you while in the water, but will help you stay buoyant. Also make sure you have it buckled in only one spot (chest or waist) and that you have easy access to the clasp and can release it immediately if necessary.
- **Stay alert.** Always be prepared for the possibility of falling through the ice. Your muscles will cramp when they hit the cold water and you will

lose your breath in shock. Read "Getting out of a hole in the ice" below, so you know exactly what to do.

- **Carry a walking stick.** See p.47. When crossing the ice, carry it like a circus tightrope walker; if you go through, it will aid in breaking your fall and keeping your head above water. It's also already in position to provide leverage to help you lift yourself out.

- **Keep tools accessible.** If you have a locking knife, screwdriver, pen or anything you can use to jam into the ice to get a grip and help pull yourself out, it won't help unless accessible within seconds. You can rig up your own self-rescue ice picks with two thin, sharp rocks or metal tent spikes connected by a metre-long string worn around your neck. Keep the string under your jacket so the picks dangle out of your jacket sleeves where they can be easily grabbed in an emergency.

- **Test the ice periodically with the walking stick.**

- **Look for weak spots.** Just because ice looks wet or weak in places doesn't mean it is all unsafe. Ice is almost always thinner along the shore, under overhanging trees and under bridges. Always use extreme caution in those areas. Look ahead for any dark or wet spots in the ice and snow.

- **Follow a leader.** If you are travelling with another person or group, let the most athletic person lead the way with the walking stick, and everyone else follow their tracks, with about 5–10m between each person. The second in line should have rope handy if available. If there's more than one rope, both the leader and the person second in line should be carrying it.

- **Listen and react.** If you feel dramatic cracks or feel the ice sag under you, drop to your hands and knees and crawl back in the direction you came from. Use your walking stick to help distribute your weight.

## Getting out of a hole in the ice

1. **Breathe steadily.** Counter the shock of the cold water with some relaxed breaths.
2. **Turn to face the direction you entered from.** That's where you know the ice will support you. The quality of the ice ahead is unknown.
3. **Shed water weight.** Use your elbows to lift you up on the edge and let the water drain from your clothes for a few moments to reduce extra weight.
4. **Dig in.** Unclip your watch or necklace, or grab keys or a locking knife – anything to help you dig into the ice.

5.  **Pull yourself out and kick.**
6.  **Stay flat.** Once on the surface do not stand. Keep your weight distributed over a wider area by rolling or sliding away from the hole.
7.  **Find land.** Get to shore (and out of the wind). Roll in snow and brush off to get dry. If shore is more than 100–200m away, do this on firm ice and put on warm clothes if available.
8.  **Warm up.** Make a fire as quickly as possible and try to prepare something warm to drink. The colder it is, the less time you have before you lose the ability to think clearly, or to use your hands effectively and, eventually, lose consciousness. You've got about 3hr at 0°C, significantly less at colder temperatures. Stay active to get warm – gathering firewood is a productive aerobic activity.
9.  **Rest.** Once you get warmed up, relax. Your body needs to recover.

### Rescuing someone who has fallen through the ice

*   **Keep your distance.** Throw them a rope, strong tree branch, scarf or belt. If necessary, tie things together so you can keep your distance.
*   **Prepare to get wet.** If it's necessary to get close, quickly make available anything you'll need to help pull yourself out if you happen to go through, such as a set of keys or a knife. If your clothes are well waterproofed inside your pack, or your pack is large and heavy, remove it first.
*   **Stay flat.** If you're using a belt or your hands to help someone out, approach the hole on your stomach. Have someone else lie stomach down and hold on to your ankles.

## Crossing a river alone

Avoid crossing rivers if possible; fast-moving water is deceptively dangerous. Don't enter the water unless you know the depth of the deepest part.

*   **Find a good crossing point.** Walk upstream (if possible) to find one. Rivers pick up water from various little streams as they head downhill, so are smallest at higher elevations.
*   **Stick to the river bed.** Don't use logs and stones to hop across, especially those that are wet.
*   **Prepare your backpack.** Release the waist belt and loosen the shoulders slightly so you can ditch it if you fall in.
*   **Face upstream and sidestep across the river.**
*   **Use a good walking stick for support.**

# Crossing a river in a group

### With rope

1. Make the rope into a giant loop.
2. Two people should hold the loop and stand on shore about 10–15m apart, while the best swimmer in the group gets inside the loop, keeping the rope in front of him as he crosses. If the person slips while crossing he can be pulled back to shore.
3. Once across, the person should hold the rope on the opposite bank, and the rope should be pulled taut between him and one of those remaining on the other side. All remaining persons bar one can cross using the rope as a guide.
4. The last person now gets inside the loop and crosses as the first person did, with two people standing 10–15m apart on the other side of the river.

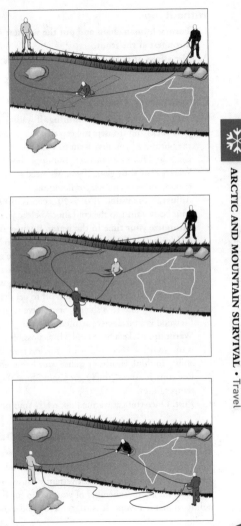

### Without rope

1. **Form a human chain and put the weakest in the middle and the strongest at the front.**
2. **Use sticks or poles.** You can use sturdy sticks like ropes to help people cross narrow bits of fast-moving water.

## Crossing freezing water

- **Think about shoes and clothing.** If wading across shallow water, remove your socks and trousers to keep them dry, but, depending on how rocky the bottom is, you may want to wear your boots for protection. Keep a jacket and hat on to protect your upper body.
- **Waterproof your gear.** If you will need to swim, place your clothes in two plastic bags and use for flotation.
- **Adjust to the water.** Take 5–10 seconds in a safe area of the water to let your body adjust to the cold shock before you go too deep.
- **Minimize your time in the water.** If you're submerged in water that is 4°C (or below) you can become too numb to help yourself in just a few minutes. You may be unconscious in as little as 12min. Keep as much of your body out of the water as possible and keep your head covered. See p.126 for other tips for surviving in freezing water.
- **Dry off.** Roll in snow and brush off to get dry. Put on dry clothes immediately and seek shelter. Stay active to get warm – gathering firewood is a productive aerobic activity.
- **Warm up.** Make a fire as quickly as possible and try to prepare something warm to drink. The colder it is, the less time you have before you lose the ability to think clearly, or to use your hands effectively and, eventually, lose consciousness. You've got about 3hr at 0°C, significantly less at colder temperatures.
- **Rest.** Once you get warmed up, relax. Your body needs to recover.

## Walking up or down a loose rocky slope

Rock fields don't represent as much danger for solo travellers as they do for a group, in which anyone can inadvertently cause a rock to tumble down the slope and hit another member of your group further below. Stay together tightly so that if anyone does trigger a rockslide, there's less likelihood of getting hit.

# Glaciers

Glaciers are dangerous and should be avoided when possible, but can be crossed with extreme caution. The danger can be reduced by crossing in a group and with proper equipment (rope, ice axe, crampons, etc).

## Crossing alone

- **Walk slowly, take your time.**
- **Carry a stick and probe the ground with each few steps.**

## Crossing in a group

- **If you have two ropes:** each member of the group should tie the rope to their harness (or around the waist if no harness is available), so all are connected. If there are only two people, try to leave 20–30m of rope between you; for three or more, keep 8–15m between each person. Tie a butterfly knot (see p.189) in one rope every few metres. The knots will help break your fall as they jam into the lip of the crevasse, but can make it difficult to pull people out. The second rope can be lowered down in this instance.
- **If you have one rope:** simply rope up leaving the distances between people as specified above.
- **Do not hold the rope slack in your hand.** Keep the rope between people fairly tight and move at the same pace. Those at the ends should keep any extra rope tucked away.
- **The lead walker should carry a stick and probe the ground with each few steps.**
- **Be prepared for a sudden fall of those around you.** If this happens, turn towards the person falling, spread your legs, dig in your heels and lean backwards to maintain control. Try not to let yourself fall forwards.

# Pulling someone out of a crevasse when connected by rope

- **Secure the rope.** If you have a stick or ice axe, dig a hole in the snow beside you with your free hand (or with the help of a third person). Secure the section of rope left over around the object.
- **Remove yourself from the rope system** so you're no longer attached to the person dangling in the crevasse.
- **Lower them down more rope.** Use a second rope or, if there's

enough, the extra part of the first rope. Have them secure it to their waist with a knot.

- **Strengthen the edge of the crevasse.** Place a backpack or firm object across the lip of the crevasse before you start pulling them up so the rope doesn't dig through the snow.

## Climbing out of a narrow crevasse

- **Locate the best conditions.** Find a spot where the walls of the crevasse are between 0.5m and 1.5m wide, all the way up.
- **Plan your route.** You may need to work your way to one side or change positions to take advantage of the changing width of the crevasse.
- **Test your skills at lower levels.** Try both techniques below and see which feels more comfortable before you start climbing.
  - **Press your back against one wall and push outward with your hands.** Take small steps and inch your back up as you go, maintaining good pressure. Even if you climb with the technique below, you can use this position to take a rest.
  - **Press one foot against the wall behind you and one against the wall in front of you and use your hands to brace, one on each wall.** When you have a good arm brace, move your legs up, then rest your arms. Alternate arms and legs.

▲ Crevasse climb, method 1    ▲ Crevasse climb, method 2

## Climbing up a rope

The prussiking technique is useful if you need to climb straight up a rope. It may come in handy going up a big tree or overhang where there's a rope in place.

**Time:** 5–10min for prussik knots and harness.

**Gear:**

- One 1.5–2-metre-long piece of rope for foot loop and prussik knot (shoelace will suffice in an emergency, but can tighten around the rope and be difficult to slide up).
- One 2–2.5-metre-long piece of rope for harness loop and prussik knot. If you don't have enough rope, make a second foot loop.

### Making a prussik climbing system

1. **Tie your long piece of rope to form a loop.** You can use the sheet knot (see p.188) or bowline (see p.189).
2. **Make a prussik knot on the rope you wish to climb up.**

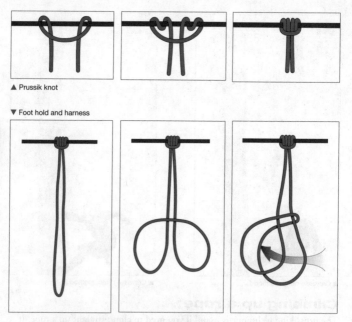

▲ Prussik knot

▼ Foot hold and harness

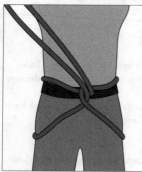

3. **Fold the other end of the loop over on itself to form a loop for your harness.** Make it big enough to step through, lift it up to your waist, then pull to tighten.
4. **Tie your short piece of rope to form a loop.**
5. **Make a prussik knot on the rope you wish to climb, below the prussik knot of the short rope.**
6. **Fold the other end over on itself to form a loop as you did with the harness loop.** Place your foot in it and pull to tighten. This should keep your foot from slipping out.

### Climbing

1. Put your weight on your foot loop.
2. Loosen the prussik knot attched to your harness loop and slide that up the rope.
3. Pull to tighten the knot, then transfer your weight to your harness as you take the weight off your foot.
4. Loosen the prussik knot attached to your foot loop and slide that up the rope.
5. Pull to tighten the knot, then transfer your weight back to your foot.

## Climbing down a rock face with just a rope

This method is not good for sheer drops, but will allow you to abseil (rappel) down a steep face.

- **Secure the rope.** Double your rope and place the middle part around a smooth rock or sturdy tree. Make sure it can't get wedged into a crack and that it won't slip over the top.
- **If you have gloves, use at least one to keep your hands from getting chafed,**

but test the grip first.
- Pass the doubled rope between your legs and over your right hip and across your chest, continuing around the back of your neck and out to your right arm.
- Keep one foot on either side of the rope as you back over the edge of the cliff.
- **Use your right arm to control the speed of your descent.** Your left holds the rope in front of you for balance.
- **Lean back and take small steps down the cliff face.**

## Stopping a slide down a snowy slope

It's a good idea to practise these methods on a small hill before you actually encounter a snowy slope – you don't want your life to depend on it when you try it for the first time.

### With an ice axe or stick
- Face uphill, feet pointed down the hill and your face towards the snow.

- **Drag the axe.** Grip it in both hands and drag it like an anchor. Keep it close to your body and push your body weight onto it.

## Without an ice axe or stick
- Use the same positioning as with ice axe.
- Spread your legs slightly for balance.
- **Dig your toes and elbows into the snow.** Arch your back to put pressure on these points.

## Driving on snow and ice
- **Go slow.** Even four-wheel drive doesn't keep you from sliding off the road on curves.
- **Pump the brake.** Short taps to the brake will keep the wheels from locking up and sending the vehicle into an uncontrolled slide. Downshift and let the engine help slow the vehicle as well.
- **If possible practise first.** Take a few mid-speed curves and slides to get a feel for the traction.
- **Keep an eye on a temperature gauge in the mountains.** Wet roads can

# Plane crash in the mountains

*Thirty-three-year-old Peter DeLeo was piloting a small single-engine plane, taking two passengers on an aerial photography trip over the snowy Sierra Nevada mountain range in California in winter. What began as a patch of turbulence led to a 1000-metre drop and, unable to regain altitude, he made a crash landing in the mountains. All three survived the landing – barely. Peter escaped through the skylight by head-butting it repeatedly and he emerged from the wreckage with seven broken ribs (preventing him from fully inflating his right lung), four breaks in his right shoulder, a torn rotator cuff, five separate fractures in his left ankle, and temporary blindness in one eye.*

*It was decided that the passengers would stay with the plane, live on the remaining supplies, build a shelter from parts of the plane and try to signal rescuers with an emergency locator transmitter, while Peter would go for help with no food, gear nor a map – just the clothes on his back. His ankle was so swollen he couldn't even tie his left boot. "After wiping the blood off my face with a handful of snow, one of my passengers looked me in the eye and asked, 'If you go, can you make it?' I paused, then said, "Yes, but it's not going to happen overnight."*

*Peter began heading south, following a stream and improvising shelter. Shivering at night inside caves and on ridges and sometimes in holes scratched out beneath a fallen tree on beds made from pine needles, he performed exercises to ward off hypothermia. Each day, he removed his clothes to allow them to dry in the sun. To stay hydrated he ate snow and ice during the daytime only when he was warm enough to digest it. Sometimes he ate bug-and-snow slushies. "I started moving before sunrise everyday so I could walk across the frozen snow crust and still have time to stop and dry my clothes at midday. You have to plan your day around your survival chores, and do them. You must discipline yourself and pace your journey. That's what keeps you alive."*

*Without the use of one eye, his depth perception was impaired. Further slowing his progress was a two-day whiteout that dumped*

1.5m of snow, trapping him in the shelter of a half-dead sequoia. Frostbite threatened his extremities, his shattered ankle drove shards of pain up his leg with every step. "The pain lets you know you're alive. I tried to accept the pain and focus on my breathing." He found a hot spring that provided him with temporary warmth and insects to eat (scavenged from under loose sections of tree bark), but malnutrition was wearing him down. He only managed to sleep only twice: once wrapped in a dirty carpet in an abandoned cabin after a day in the hot spring, and again in an old, rank outhouse.

Peter trudged onward in waist-deep snow and managed to cross two peaks – one at 3660m – on sheer willpower, and avert the curiosity of bears by singing pop tunes. He gave up his plan to follow the Kern River and headed east, staying high up on the sunny southern peaks, trying to take advantage of the direct sunlight in the mountains, hoping to make it to Highway 395 on the eastern slope of the California Sierras.

"Along the way, I started seeing the forest through a different set of eyes – instead of trees, rocks and bushes being obstacles that I had to hike around or over, I now saw them as potential food sources and materials to make shelter."

Meanwhile, search planes flew overhead, unable to find the lost plane. Several times Peter frantically tried to signal the planes and helicopters – one even passed just 15m away – but without any luck.

Thirteen days and over 70km into his survival trek, he had lost over 20kg. It was then, just as he caught sight of the highway he was hoping to find, that a snow-slide swept him off a cliff and left him dangling by his one good arm.

When he finally reached the highway, he found it almost impossible to stop cars and just as difficult to convince the authorities that he was the lost pilot who had been all but given up for dead.

Fully recovered today, Peter has re-trekked his survival route and written the book Survive: My Fight for Life in the High Sierras, detailing his journey out of the mountains.

suddenly become ice within minutes. Heading up into higher altitudes or down into cold valleys can both cause this.

- **Descending a steep hill should be done carefully.** Plot your route and where you can go at the bottom if the vehicle gets going too fast. Keep your speed in check with the gears and accelerate slightly if the rear starts to slide around.

## Driving across water

- **Coat engine electronics with oil from the dipstick or use a lubricant spray.**
- **Open doors and windows to allow water in.** If you don't, there's a good chance the vehicle will float away.
- **Drive slowly and maintain speed.**
- **Be prepared for bumps.** The road may be washed out beneath the water, even if the water looks calm.
- **See p.85 for driving in deep ruts.**

# Hazards

## Avalanches

### Avoiding avalanches

- Avalanches rarely occur with less than 30cm of snow.
- Avalanches occur on 30- to 45-degree slopes.
- Risk of avalanche is lowest in the early morning.
- Try to stay among trees during the descent of a snowy slope, where the risk of an avalanche is lower.
- Go down (or across) a snowy slope one at a time so if one person gets caught in an avalanche the others can assist in the rescue.

### Surviving an avalanche

If you're carrying proper equipment (avalanche beacons, probes and shovels) you should practise using them before heading into a danger area.

- **Don't try to outrun it.** Cut across and down. Try to turn off into a tree-filled area if you're on an open slope.

- **If caught by the avalanche, swim.** Use a freestyle swimming motion to try to stay on the surface.
- **Create breathing space.** Avalanches solidify quickly the moment they stop. As you get covered, use your hands to create a breathing space in front of your face.
- **Orient yourself.** Drool a bit to see which way is down, then dig upward as quickly as possible – avalanche snow solidifies by the second.

## Waiting out a blizzard

Moving in a blizzard with no visibility is very dangerous.
- **Try to find natural shelter from the wind and snow.** If none is available, dig a trench.
- **Keep your eyes covered.** If you don't have adequate goggles or glasses (see p.45), stinging snow particles can cause snow blindness (see p.66) – wrap a scarf (or anything similar) over your eyes.

## Bears

Different breeds of bear will act differently when encountering a human. To be on the safe side, treat all bears with the same degree of caution. Being inside a vehicle doesn't always guarantee safety as some bears are strong enough to force entry; it's best to keep the windows up and doors shut and keep moving. Don't forget to remove food when your vehicle is parked; bears have been known to break into cars for food – and trash them in the process.

### General precautions
- **Announce your arrival.** Try talking or singing while you walk to avoid surprising a bear. Many have found ringing a "bear bell" easier and more effective.
- **Don't sleep in the same clothes you use for cooking.** You don't want an extra dose of food perfume on if a bear comes sniffing around your tent.
- **Store food and garbage safely.** Hoist it between two trees with rope (not straight up a tree where a bear can climb to it). And make sure it's not hanging above your camping area. Do not keep any food in your tent.
- **Don't hike with dogs.** Dogs have been known to antagonize bears.
- **Hike with bear spray.** Make sure you've packed it so you can reach it in seconds.

## If you see a bear at a distance (over 400m)

- Head back the way you came (or alter your course) until the bear is out of sight.
- If you need to return, wait 20min and make plenty of noise as you do.

## If you encounter a defensive bear at close range

A bear will be defensive if you catch it by surprise.

- **Don't run.** Bears are much faster than you and are more likely to attack if you run than if you stay still.
- **Stick together.** A group or couple should stand together, with arms in the air to look bigger.
- **Be quiet, don't make eye contact, don't kneel down or turn your back.**
- **Use bear spray if available.** Consider wind direction when doing so.
- **If the bear is far enough away and everyone can climb a tree, do so.** If everyone can't, stay together on the ground.
- **Try to determine if the bear is acting aggressively.** A defensive bear can be quick to attack.
- **Fight back if attacked.** Go for the eyes and snout with a hiking stick and keep shouting at the bear.
- **Slowly back away while facing the bear.**

## If you encounter an offensive bear at close range

An offensive bear is one that follows you, moves toward you or wanders into your camp. Treat the bear as you would a defensive one (see above) but in addition:

- **Make loud noises.** A compressed air horn is ideal, but whistling and yelling are also effective.
- **Consider the possibility of mock charges.** Don't fire your bear spray prematurely. You've got only about 9 seconds' worth. If the bear is charging fast but you can see his ears stand up and his posture is not too low to the ground, it's likely to be a mock charge. Once he stops, be patient and still for a while and see if he wanders off. If not, very, very slowly, start backing away while speaking to him in a calm, monotone voice.
- **Play dead if attacked.** Don't fight back. Keep your backpack on and cover your neck and head. A curious bear is typically not out to kill. Many lose interest and leave.

# Medical issues

## Frostbite

Frostbite, freezing of the skin and underlying tissues, typically affects extremities (especially the fingers, toes, nose and ears). The area feels numb and the skin looks white (bluish black in advanced cases).

### Avoiding frostbite

- **Monitor your extremities, which are typically the first to freeze.** Deal with each vulnerable body part: face (warm with hands, twitch and make faces), ears (warm with hands, keep completely covered), hands (make fists inside your gloves, place under armpits to warm, swing arms aggressively to get blood to fingertips), feet (wiggle toes inside boots, stomp, balance against a tree and swing each leg separately to help blood move to your feet).
- **Try to keep hands and feet dry.**
- **Stay hydrated and eat plenty.**
- **Avoid tight-fitting gloves and socks.** Don't put on an extra layer of socks if your boots are already snug.

**Once skin becomes cold or numb:**
- **Swing your arms in circles.** This forces warm blood out to your hands.
- **Swing your legs, one at a time.** Hold onto something for balance.
- **Place your hands under your armpits to warm them.**
- **Place your feet under someone else's armpits.**

### Treating frostbite

- **Do not use frostbitten body parts (if it is avoidable).** They will swell when thawed and are more susceptible to refreezing and further damage. You can walk on frostbitten feet, but not once you've warmed them.
- **Warm slowly.** Put the frostbitten body part in lukewarm (not hot) water or apply lukewarm compress for 20min. If warm water is not available, apply warm, dry clothing and blankets to the affected area. Avoid direct strong heat, such as fires and chemically activated hot pads and hot water bottles.
- **Take pain medication if available.**
- **Do not rub the skin.**
- **Apply sterile dressings, wrap carefully, keep warm.**

# Hypothermia

Hypothermia, which is the profound cooling of the body's torso to below 35.5°C, doesn't just occur in extreme winter conditions. You can experience it while hiking on a mild day if it starts to rain, then gets windy, and you're not wearing adequate clothing.

## Treating hypothermia

- **Do not massage extremities.**
- **Stay hydrated and eat plenty.**
- **Modify environment.** Shivering is the safest and most effective means of rewarming when a person is mildly hypothermic, but should warn you to improve insulation, get out of the wind, into dry clothes or to cuddle up to a warm person.
- **Rewarm slowly.** Preferably in a tub of lukewarm (not hot) water, but keep extremities out of the tub to keep blood vessels from dilating and allowing the cooled blood to rush back to the heart and trigger a heart attack. If no warm water is available, find shelter and build a fire. Take care with the fire heat: someone with hypothermia should not be standing in front of a roaring fire.
- **Use body heat.** Without a fire, zip two sleeping bags together and put one person on either side of the victim to warm them with body heat. This is most effective when all have removed clothes. With only one sleeping bag, put the victim in and take turns squeezing others in, rotating people to make the most of the collective body heat. With just one person, that person is also at risk of cooling down to hypothermic levels, so they should stay aware of their own body temperature and limit their contact.
- **Increase sugar intake.**

# Sun and snow blindness

Symptoms of sun blindness include burning, watery eyes, decreased vision and a scratchy feeling (as though sand were present in the eyes). Snow blindness is when your eyes water and freeze. For advice on avoiding sun and snow blindness see p.45.

## Treating sun and snow blindness

Depending on how serious your exposure, it could take up to 24hr for noticeable improvement.

- **Cover eyes with wet cloth unless temperature is below freezing.**
- **Cover both eyes and keep eyes closed so as not to expose to any light.**
- **Use an eye lubricant for soothing effect.**
- **Seek professional help as soon as possible.**

## Immersion foot (trench foot)

This results from over 48hr of exposure to water. The feet gradually go numb and the skin turns red or blue. If untreated, the foot could turn gangrenous and result in amputation.

### Avoiding immersion foot

- **Keep your feet as dry as possible.**
- **Change socks at least daily, preferably two or three times a day when damp.** Let the wet ones air out on your pack or against your body.
- **Remove shoes when crossing small streams.** If you keep your shoes on because of rocks, remove socks first.
- **Let your feet breathe at regular intervals.** Taking off your shoes is especially important if you have only one pair of socks. Do this at midday in direct sunlight.
- **Use talc or baby powder to soak up moisture.**

### Treating immersion foot

1. **Warm the affected area in warm water (about 37°C).** This will help relieve the pain.
2. **Dry the area thoroughly and keep it clean.**
3. **Elevate the feet to reduce swelling.**
4. **Keep the entire body warm to improve circulation.**
5. **Take a non-steroidal, anti-inflammatory medication such as ibuprofen.**

## Altitude sickness

Altitude sickness is intolerance to low oxygen environments at elevation, typically from a lack of acclimatization. This is more dangerous than most people realize, and should be treated seriously.

### Avoiding altitude sickness

- **Ascend at a rate that gives your body time to acclimatize.** People acclimatize at different rates, but in general, the following guidelines will work:
  - Above 3000m your sleeping elevation should not increase more than 300m per night.
  - Every 1000m you should spend a second night at the same elevation.
- **Consider using medication.** Diamox (acetazolamide) is most useful as an altitude-sickness preventive. Take 125mg (half a tablet) twice a day for 2 days at sea level a few weeks prior to heading up to higher elevations. If you experience major side effects such as vomiting, rashes or confusion, stop taking the drug (tingling of fingers and feet are common but harmless). If your body accepts the drug, take 125mg (half a tablet) twice a day for 3 days before staying at 3500m and continue the same dose for 2 or 3 days until you feel acclimatized. Do not take for more than 5 days total. This drug is not a necessary precaution or preventative, but may be useful for people flying directly to high-altitude destinations such as La Paz, Bolivia or Lhasa, Tibet.
- **Take coca leaves.** In parts of South America coca leaves, kept in the cheek like chewing tobacco or infused and drunk as tea, have also been credited with aiding high-altitude ailments and do not cause the sort of mind-altering effects of the plant's derivatives, crack or cocaine.

### Treating altitude sickness

Without medication, the basic remedy for nausea, headache, dizziness or light-headedness is to stop moving, and head down to lower altitude and acclimatize if the symptoms don't go away after a rest. It doesn't mean making a beeline for the bottom. Usually, the symptoms will abate after just a little descent, and you may even be able to continue once your body has adjusted at its own pace. Medication for the following two conditions can be taken at once if unsure of diagnosis.

> We do not recommend taking prescription medication unless it has been prescribed specifically for you. However, in an emergency situation you may feel there is no alternative, in which case the information here can be used as a guide. Medications such as those listed on the opposite page do not fix the problem so that you can push on to the summit; they buy you some time until you can get down to lower elevation and find professional medical help.

ARCTIC AND MOUNTAIN SURVIVAL • Medical issues

### High Altitude Cerebral Edema (HACE)

One indication of severe HACE is if a person can't walk heel to toe, but they may also be suffering from an incapacitating headache – one that won't go away with over-the-counter headache medication (a good first step) – possibly accompanied by vomiting.

*   **Treat with the steriod dexamethasone (Decadron).** Take an 8mg (tablet) dose, followed by 4mg every 6hr. This should decrease the swelling of the brain.
*   **Treatment should last for one day, not exceeding a total of 20mg in 24hr.**
*   **If the symptoms persist, head to low altituide and seek professional medical help.**
*   **Side effects include gastric bleeding and mood swings (feeling excited, confused or "high").**

### High Altitude Pulmonary Edema (HAPE)

Severe HAPE is typically recognized with breathlessness and crackly or bubbling chest noise. In mild cases it will begin to appear as a dry cough.

*   **Give oxygen and move to low altitude.**
*   **Treat with nifedipine.** Take 20mg (slow release capsules) immediately and 20mg every 6hr for 1 day. Treat even if in doubt of diagnosis. Side effects can include a sudden drop in blood pressure. If you feel faint, lie down.

*This chapter was written in consultation with:*

**Brian Horner**, *an Alaskan-based survival instructor at LRT Training systems (Ⓦ www.survivaltraining.com), a professional mountain guide and member of the Alaskan Mountain rescue group.*

**Mors Kochanski**, *a Canadian survival instructor at Karamat (Ⓦ www.karamat .com) and author of* Bushcraft *and several other books.*

**Dr David E. Johnson**, *an emergency physician who currently serves as the president and medical director of Wilderness Medical Associates (Ⓦ www.wildmed .com). David supervises over a hundred faculty members, teaching medical courses to backcountry enthusiasts and professionals around the globe. He also co-wrote* The Wilderness Medical Associates Wilderness First Aid Guide.

**Kevin Frey**, *Grizzly bear management specialist for Yellowstone Ecosystem, Montana Fish, Wildlife and Parks.*

# Desert survival

# Desert survival

# Desert survival

Deserts cover approximately one fifth of the earth's surface and although they are arid environments (receiving less than 25cm of rain annually) they're not all Lawrence-of-Arabia-style dunes that stretch to the horizon. Deserts may also be barren hills, salt marshes, flat grasslands and mountains separated by dry, flat basins – at times more than 1000m above sea level and subject to flash floods. Daytime temperatures in deserts can rise above 50°C in the shade and nighttime temperatures can drop below freezing. A difference of 30°C between day and night is not uncommon.

If nothing else, make sure you bear in mind these basic **rules to live by** in the desert:

- Stay out of the sun as much as possible. This includes covering your skin.
- Travel at dawn, dusk, and at night by moonlight. Rest in the shade when it's too hot.
- Keep hydrated and conserve water. Breathe through your nose.
- Pay attention to your environment. Utilize every possible resource.
- If you're expecting a search party, be sure to mark your trail and leave signals.

# Basic needs

## Water

Your water requirements are a combination of air temperature and physical activity. You can't train your body to require less water but you can minimize your efforts and keep your body as cool as possible.

### Conserving water

- **Only travel at dawn, dusk, and by moonlight.** The air is cooler so you'll sweat less and avoid the harsh rays of the sun. Spend the hottest part of the day (roughly 10am to 4pm) resting in the shade.
- **Don't sit directly on the ground when resting in extremely hot conditions.** Try to find a log or branch since rocks and sand on the ground retain the sun's heat and can be as much as 20–30 degrees hotter than the air temperature during daylight hours.

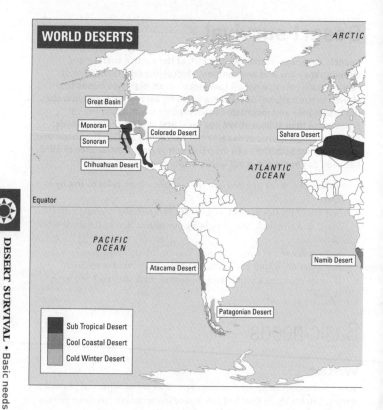

WORLD DESERTS

ARCTIC

Great Basin

Monoran

Sonoran

Colorado Desert

Chihuahuan Desert

Sahara Desert

ATLANTIC
OCEAN

Equator

PACIFIC
OCEAN

Atacama Desert

Namib Desert

Patagonian Desert

Sub Tropical Desert
Cool Coastal Desert
Cold Winter Desert

- **Avoid comfort vices.** Alcohol and cigarettes contribute to dehydration.
- **Wear clothing that covers as much of your skin as possible.** A hat, long-sleeved shirt and trousers will slow the evaporation of your sweat and keep you from getting sunburnt.
- **Don't eat if water is limited.** Your body uses water for digestion of food. Sugars are better than carbohydrates, but it's better to minimize all food consumption.

OCEAN

Kyzyl-Kum Desert

Kara-Kum Desert

Gobi Desert

Iranian Desert

Taklamakan Desert

PACIFIC OCEAN

Thar Desert

Arabian Desert

INDIAN OCEAN

Great Sandy Desert

Gibson Desert

Great Victoria

Kalahari Desert

- **Breathe through your nose and speak as little as possible.** This helps keep valuable body moisture from evaporating.
- **Don't over-ration water.** You shouldn't drink yourself full, nor should you hold back too much. Even with a limited supply, take sips at regular intervals to keep cool and reduce sweating. Conserve your fluids by reducing activity during the heat of day. For extreme situations, see p.130.

# In a desert emergency

1. **Get yourself and any companions out of harm's way.**
2. **Address any acute medical problems.** See the medical appendix on pp.171–186.
3. **Take a deep breath and get your bearings.** Don't underestimate the importance of conquering fear and anxiety. See p.186 to help establish your survival mindset. Look for any footprints or tyre tracks that will allow you to retrace your route easily.
4. **Keep hydrated.** Your need for water is vital in a warm environment. See below for ways to get water and p.89 for dehydration signs and cure.
5. **Shelter.** Many deserts can drop below freezing at night, so don't underestimate the risk of exposure. Make certain you're out of the wind, even if you need to dig a trench to ensure this.
6. **Build a fire.** It will provide warmth, morale, a rescue signal and will enable you to purify water. See p.198 for fire starting and p.38 for maintaining body heat.
7. **Plan.** Now that you've dealt with the most pressing issues, read through this entire chapter and cross-referenced sections to prepare more thoroughly for survival. Decide whether you will wait to be rescued or if it will be beneficial to attempt to leave your immediate environment. If in doubt, stay put. Another option for a group is to send one or two pairs of fit volunteers in search of help (in different directions) while the rest of the group remains in place.
   **Reasons to stay put**
   - People are likely to be looking for you.
   - The vehicle you were travelling in or your immediate terrain means that you will be easily spotted from the air.
   - The terrain, weather or injuries will hinder movement.
   - The visibility is poor.

## Finding water

Major sources

- **Follow animal trails.** When they converge, chances are the larger, more trafficked trails lead to water.
- **Look to the sky.** Flocks of birds typically circle over waterholes at dusk.
- **Listen and look for bugs and bees.** They can often be found near a water source.

- You don't have a map/GPS equipment and can't work out the way to civilization.
- The sun will soon set.

**If you stay put**
- Set up a signal (see p.89).
- Scavenge for supplies.
- Improve shelter to increase chances of prolonged sleep.
- Once camp is set up, conserve energy by staying very still while you wait for rescuers to spot your signals.

**Reasons to move**
- The terrain you are in is dangerous (due to avalanche, rock slides, animals, etc) or is exposed to the elements.
- You have navigation equipment, necessary gear to handle the terrain, and can determine a realistic route to safety.
- It is unlikely that anyone is looking for you.

**If you move**
- Check around to see if there is anything you can take with you that might aid in survival.
- Leave a clue about which direction you're heading in – logs or rocks forming an arrow – in case anyone shows up. As you progress, leave a trail that could be followed; piles of rocks, for example. Make sure you can use this trail to find your way back to your starting point, too.
- Put something shiny on your pack or hat (such as a CD or aluminium foil) to attract attention of search crews.
- Don't waste time foraging for food (it's not initially important), but do keep an eye out for known, convenient food sources as you go. See p.81 for food gathering.
- Dress appropriately for desert conditions (see p.79).
- Keep a fire going at night when you stop (search crews may search at night with night-vision goggles).

- **Look for large, green leafy trees.** If there's one such tree in the middle of a field of smaller bushes or lower, less leafy trees, water is most likely to be near the large, leafy tree.
- **Look for dry river beds in the morning.** Some run with water in the early hours before nearby trees begin to "drink".

### From the ground

Dig 30–60-centimetre-deep holes in the following spots to find water. If there's no water, wait two minutes for water to start seeping in before you move on to another spot.

**Places to dig:**

- **Near green vegetation.**
- **Where there's damp surface sand.**
- **At the base of cliffs and large rock outcroppings.**
- **In the outer curves of dry river beds.** With this you may need to wait an hour for the water to fill the hole (if there is any).

### From plants

- **Cut the top off a barrel cactus and mash the pulp.** This can be done in a can or while still in the cactus using a stick or your fist. Soak up the liquid using a cloth that you can wring out in your mouth. Sucking up the liquid through a straw, pipe or tube also works.
- **Collect moisture from plants.** During the day, place a plastic bag over as much green foliage as possible on a lush bush or tree that's exposed to direct sunlight. Tighten the bag around the branch and seal with string or wire or tie the bag's edges together. In a few hours, the moisture will have collected. If you're on the move, cut as many leafy branches as you can fit into your plastic bag, seal it closed, and carry it for a few hours until the moisture has perspired. Caution: do not do this with toxic plants (see p.197 for testing for poison) or near the ocean (salty water).

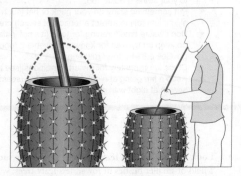

# Maintaining your body temperature

- **Stay hydrated.**
- **Keep yourself covered.** Resist the urge to strip down when it gets hot.
- **Wear loose, baggy clothes.**
- **Wear a hat.** Protect the back of your neck with a cloth. Tuck a bandana under the edges of your hat to create a "desert hat".
- **Stay out of the sun.** Walk and search for water or food only at dawn, dusk, night and in the shade.
- **Don't walk barefoot or cut holes in your shoes.** Stop regularly to cool and dry your feet and let your socks dry.

# Shelter

Try to conserve energy (and water) by taking advantage of your natural surroundings. When building shelters, try to create "double shade" – two layers of material between you and the sun with at least 30cm of space between them. This can reduce the temperature inside your shelter by 11–22°C.

## Natural shelters

- **Maintain a lookout for natural shade.** A large tree, cave or rock overhang is ideal.
- **Add a simple roof.** If natural shade is unavailable, look for a gap between large stones and weigh down a tarp, poncho or jacket with rocks or sand to provide some cover. Without a synthetic cover, lay down branches or sticks to make a roof.

## Shade tent

**Time:** 5–15min
**Gear:**
- One 2-metre piece of rope or cord.
- A few sticks.
- 1 of the following: tarp, poncho, sheet or large plastic bag.
- **Make any of the illustrated tents.** See overleaf.
- **Minimize sun exposure.** If wind isn't a factor, in the northern hemisphere, make the shelter's opening face north. In the southern hemisphere, make it face south. This will minimize exposure to the sun as it arcs across the sky during the hottest part of the day.

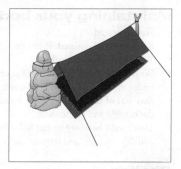

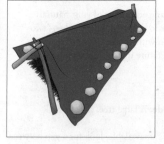

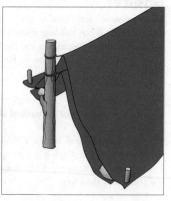

- **Minimize wind exposure.** If windy, make sure the opening faces downwind and the edges of the cover are well secured.

## Sand cave

**Time:** 20–60min
**Gear:** 1 of the following: tarp/ about 20 sticks/several leafy branches
1. **Dig a trench in the sand.** It should be about 1m deep and slightly wider, and 1m longer, than the person/s

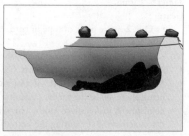

▲ Sand cave, side view

who will lie in it. Pile the sand evenly around three of the sides.

2. **Cover the trench with a tarp, sticks, or leafy branches.** Use sand and rocks to weigh down the edges and hold the roof in place.

3. **Make an extra roof.** Pile sand 30cm higher on the edges and add a second roof to increase cooling. If you are using a tarp and it's large enough, fold it in half and use one half for each layer, with air space in between.

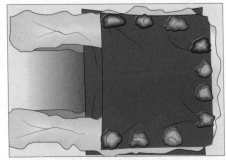

▲ Sand cave (double layer tarp), top view

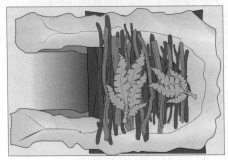

▲ Sand cave (tarp and foliage), top view

## Finding food

### Plants

The grasses in deserts (except the Sahara and Gobi) are edible. The three most available and easily identifiable desert plants are the cattail, thistle and prickly pear cactus. If unsure about the plant, beware of any milky sap and use the poison test on p.197.

#### Cactus fruit and leaves

The edible fruit – 5 to 9cm long and shaped like an avocado with thick skin – are mango-coloured on the outside and yellow to red on the inside. You can cut open and chomp on the nopales (cactus pads) that look like green rabbit ears. They have a soft but crunchy texture that becomes a bit sticky when

▲ Prickly pears

cooked. The taste is like that of a tart green bean or green pepper. Be sure to remove the prickly "eyes" and any remaining prickers, then cut off outside edges of the pads as well as any dry or fibrous areas.

### Insects

See pp.99–100 for insect collecting and eating.

### Animal traps

Rabbits, foxes, hedgehogs, rodents and other specially adapted mammals can be found in deserts. Lizards are typically edible (except the 30–50-centimetre-long black with yellow or pinkish Gilea monster in the southwest USA and the similar-looking, though somewhat larger and less colourful, Beaded lizard in Mexico and Central America) but are hard to catch and don't have enough meat on them to justify the energy required. For traps, see p.190.

## Fire

Deserts are not typically stocked with an abundance of firewood. If there's a nearby vehicle or plane in disrepair, oil and petrol can be drained for use as fuel. Oil can be drained from under the vehicle. Petrol can be siphoned out (with a bit of sucking) with a hose taken from the engine area.

### Petrol fire

- **Fill an empty metal can about one third full with sand.** You can also dig a hole into the hard earth and fill it a third full with sand.
- **Add gasoline and mix until the sand looks "wet".**
- **Ignite.**

▲ Petrol fire

### Oil fire

- **Place a piece of string at the bottom of an empty can.** Prop it up with a piece of metal; this forms the wick.
- **Fill can with oil until it is a few centimetres below the top of the wick, then mix in petrol or anti-freeze.**
- **Light the wick, not the oil mixture.** If you can find a long stick, dip the tip in petrol, light it, and use that to light the wick, so you don't have to get too close.

▲ Oil fire

For information on **building regular camp or signal fires** ▶ see p.198.

# Travel

## Navigating in a desert

- **Survey and map your terrain.** Do this during daylight (not the hottest part of the day) and from a nearby high vantage point. Make a note of any landmarks and look for places that might provide shelter. Memorize it if you have no pen and paper. Bear in mind that the emptiness of a desert can mean things seem up to three times nearer than they actually are.
- **Place your compass on your map and write down the direction you plan to head in.** Without a compass, use the methods on pp.191–193.
- **Start moving as the sun's heat begins to fade in the late afternoon.**
- **Move slowly and cautiously when travelling at night without moonlight.** Ravines and other geographical hazards are common in the desert.

- **Mark your trail as you go.** Use small piles of stones or insert sticks straight into the sand. Also take frequent mental snapshots: look back in the direction you've come from and survey the landscape so you can orient yourself in case you need to head back.
- **Look above mirages.** During the day, mirages can occur (the landscape about 1.5km away will appear to move and make you feel as if you are surrounded by water). If you move to a higher vantage point, many of the mirages will disappear.

## Reducing glare

Protect your eyes. Without goggles or sunglasses, you should create makeshift glasses (see p.45) to prevent sun blindness (see p.66).

## Driving in the desert

- **Carry enough water.** If you can't fit 4–5l water per passenger per day of estimated travel (plus three extra days per person) onboard, you have too many people in the vehicle.
- **Deflate the tyres to almost 50 percent of their suggested pressure when driving in sand.**
- **Don't accelerate or brake quickly.** Start slowly and maintain speed in a smooth, consistent manner that allows you to "ride up" on the sand; don't go so fast that you skip across it or so slowly that you sink into it.
- **Approach steep hills straight on.** But get out and check what's on the other side first.
- **Beware of rollovers when driving across slopes.** Most vehicles will tip over sideways on a 35–40 degree hill.
- **Park the vehicle pointing down a hill to avoid getting stuck in the sand.**
- **Carry an air bag to lift the vehicle.** A jack won't do you much good in the soft sand. The bag can be inflated by attaching it to the exhaust pipe with a hose.
- **Don't spin wheels when stuck.** If you're not getting any traction, place boards or floor mats under the tyres (or use an air pump to lift the car). You can also place branches criss-cross under the tyres or over spots ahead

For information on **picking a walking stick** ▶ see p.47, on **walking up or down a loose rocky slope** ▶ see p.52 and on **avoiding and treating snake bites** ▶ see p.111 and p.112.

of you that look as if they might give you trouble.

- **Bring extra fuel.** Driving on sand is far less fuel efficient and it's easy to underestimate how much you'll need to cover a set distance. Store the fuel outside the vehicle.

- **Pull over and stop during a dust/sand storm.** Turn on your emergency lights. Try to keep the back of the vehicle facing the storm to prevent damage to the front.

- **If you break down, don't leave the vehicle.** It's still easier to spot than you. Opening the hood and boot (trunk) is the signal for help. Build signal fires (see p.89) and stay put. Side mirrors work well for signalling. See p.195 for aiming a mirror.

- **Do not drive in deep road ruts.** The ruts can suddenly get deeper than the bottom clearance of the vehicle, which can leave you very stuck. Instead, drive so that one side of the car is between the ruts and the other is off to the side. If you do get into the ruts, constantly turn the vehicle slightly from side to side so your wheels get traction on the edges of the ruts.

- **Avoid the engine overheating.** Give the vehicle a chance to cool off (park in the shade and open the bonnet) when driving during the hottest part of the day. If there's no place to stop, slow down, turn off the AC and (strange as it may sound) switch on the heater. You'll need to roll down the windows to combat the heat.

- **Cover the vehicle when left in the sun.** If you can't park in the shade, try to cover the vehicle (and tyres) with a white sheet to prevent overheating.

- **Avoid sand and dust in the fuel tank.** When adding petrol, rig a filter or place a cloth around the opening to prevent sand and dust from entering.

# Lost in the desert

*Mauro Prosperi, a 39-year-old Italian policeman, marathon runner and Olympic pentathlete, willingly signed up for the Marathon des Sables, a gruelling seven-day, 230-kilometre run across the Sahara in 38-degree-celsius heat. It was to be a punishing experience, even by usual sand-marathon standards.*

*Mauro was running in seventh place when a windstorm swept through and masked the terrain in swirling clouds of sand. "I stopped and turned my back to the wind, then covered my face with a special sandstorm scarf and glasses. I eventually found a log to block the wind, but I needed to keep moving a bit to keep from getting buried. The storm lasted eight hours, and when the winds died down, I didn't know I was lost."*

*Mauro had a compass but no reference points and it took a while before he realized he had lost his way. "I wasn't panicked, just despaired. Fear – the type that doesn't paralyze you – is important. It forces you to think and concentrate. You need to be intelligent to survive."*

*The first thing Mauro did was urinate into a water bottle. He knew that this first urination was going to be the most clear (and most drinkable) if he didn't come across a fresh water supply. "My father taught me that trick." Mauro walked between 4.30 and 11am, then found shelter and kept out of the sun until 4.30pm.*

*After three days of wandering, taking sips of that initial urine, he was enveloped in another sandstorm that lasted for twelve hours.*

# Hazards

## Avoiding scorpion stings

- **Shake out any items (shoes, sleeping bag, sheets, clothes) that have been lying around.** Take these precautions when indoors as well, not just in camping areas.
- **Leave them be.** Scorpions will sting only when provoked. If they're in

*He found a small Muslim shrine, hung his Italian flag out front and crawled inside, where he found some nourishment. He caught two small bats, twisted off their necks and drank their blood. ("If you cook the animals, you lose the water content.") Still, he was sure he wasn't going to last much longer. "I reasoned that if I died in that shrine, my body would eventually be found. If I died while walking, my body would never be found. I wanted my family to be able to recover my body so they could come to terms with my death." He wrote a note to his wife with a piece of charcoal and then slit his wrists and waited to die. But there was a minor problem: his blood had thickened and wouldn't drain.*

*Mauro took that as a sign. "It gave me more confidence. I started to view the desert as a place where people can live. I started to think of myself as a man of the desert. I wanted to see my family and friends again and I concentrated on that." He decided again to try and walk his way out of the desert and headed for a mountain range in the distance.*

*Five days after leaving the shrine – eight days of drinking almost nothing but that urine – he found a small oasis. He resisted the temptation to splurge (and make himself ill) and instead took a reasonable, calculated amount. He continued for two more days until he happened upon some Tuareg nomads, who took him on camelback to a nearby village.*

*His quest had landed him nearly 200km to the west – in Algeria. He was 15kg lighter and his liver had been damaged, but not enough to keep him from competing in six more Marathons des Sables.*

Interview translation by Malin Edlund.

your sleeping area, however, you can shoo them away with a long, leafy branch (leafy end towards the scorpion) or broom.
• **See p.91 for treating scorpion stings.**

## Riding out a sandstorm

Sandstorms are most common in spring and autumn and typically last one to four days. The winds can reach 144kph and carry sand as much as 2m off the ground, though dust is carried as high as 5000m. Duststorms caused by strong, sustained winds may allow for more visibility, but are also a hazard.

## Desert winds

**Brickfielder** A hot, dusty wind in South Australia that blows strongly, often for several days at a time. The northern brickfielder is almost invariably followed by a strong southerly buster, cloudy and cool from the ocean.

**Haboob** A strong wind and sandstorm (or duststorm) in the northern and central Sudan, especially around Khartoum, where the average occurrence is about 24 per year. This duststorm, moving at an average speed of 50kph, can reach heights of up to 1000m. It occurs from May until September and lasts about three hours. The Haboob is common throughout the Sahara, but a version of it is known to blow through Texas and Arizona.

**Harmattan** A dry, dusty trade wind blowing off the Sahara Desert across the Gulf of Guinea and the Cape Verde Islands from December to February.

**Shamal** A May to early July northwesterly cool wind, blowing over Iraq and the Persian Gulf, often strong during the day, but decreasing at night. It can whip up a pinkish-tan dust that fills the air for days.

**Sharki** A southeasterly hot and dusty wind which sometimes blows in the Persian Gulf.

**Sirocco** A warm, dusty wind in North Africa occurring in spring and autumn (most common in March and November) that can reach speeds of 100kph. It typically lasts from half a day to several days.

- **Look for natural shelter.** The downwind side of a rock, tree or even a steep dune.
- **Move to higher ground.** Flying sand travels low. (However, do not do this if you see lightning or hear thunder, when it's better to stay low.)
- **Place a damp bandana over nose and mouth (bank-robber style).**
- **Lubricate.** Coat lips and inside of nose with a bit of petroleum jelly or lip balm.
- **Make sure your body is covered to prevent sandburn from exposure to the whipping sand.**
- **Mark your direction of travel.** Use two sticks jammed into the sand or lie down in the direction you're heading and ride out the storm. You can also use a backpack as a windbreak and point your face downwind.
- **Stay together if in a group.** Hold hands or all hold onto a rope so that no one gets lost.
- **For tips on driving in a sandstorm see p.85.**

- **Place reflective objects at different angles outside your shelter.** While on the move, put something shiny on your pack or hat (aluminium foil, CD, tin can with label removed).
- **Make smoky fires by day and bright fires at night.** Add green foliage, a log drenched in oil or an old car tyre to a roaring fire to generate smoke. Have a pile of dry kindling or a log drenched in petrol ready to increase the flame in a hurry if a plane comes by.
- **Mark the sand.** If there's no wind, and you can change the colour of the sand by kicking off the top layer, use your feet to stomp out an SOS and arrow indicating your direction.
- **See p.194 for more on signalling in general.**

# Medical issues

## Dehydration

### Avoiding dehydration

- **Drink.** If available, drink a few gulps of water every 15min. Always drink when thirsty.
- **Eat salty foods if sweating heavily and consuming large volumes of water.**
- **Stay in the shade during the hottest hours of the day.**
- **Wet your clothes and hat.** A wet bandana around the neck is effective for keeping your body temperature in check, which reduces sweating.

### Treating dehydration

If you start experiencing a dry mouth, thirst, headache and/or muscle cramps, treat for dehydration. Dark urine is also a common sign that you are not taking in enough water. See p.90 for symptoms of hyponatremia, which may occur under similar conditions.

- **Stop exertion and seek shade immediately.**
- **Drink plenty of water, preferably with rehydration mix (p.90 for forumula).**
- **Eat something salty.**

## Oral rehydration recipe

Mix one litre of purified water (see p.201 for purification) with 1tsp of salt and 8tsp of sugar until dissolved.

- **Cool off.** Wet your clothes (urine works in a jam) and have someone fan you (or move so that you're exposing yourself to the wind). If you're in a sandy area, dig down to find cooler sand and place it on key parts of your body, such as head, chest and wrists. You could also bury yourself partially in the cool sand.

## Heatstroke

If you are panting like a dog and your heart is beating rapidly, think heatstroke. Caused by a body temperature of 40.5°C or over, the condition is life-threatening and immediate cooling is necessary. Other symptoms include a swollen, red face and reddened whites of the eyes, delirium and unconsciousness. Heatstroke treatment can be initiated in the field, but a clinic that can administer an IV is a better bet.

### Treating heatstroke

1. **Cool the person immediately.** A dip in a cool stream is ideal. You can also cool with wet rags or by covering with cool sand. Cool compresses, if limited, should be applied to head, neck, armpits and crotch.
2. **Lie the person down in the shade and treat for shock (see p.173).**
3. **Fan the the patient.**
4. **Provide drinking fluids.** Water with rehydration mix is best if available.
5. **Monitor the person while cooling down.** They may vomit, have diarrhoea, shiver, struggle, slip into unconsciousness or have heart failure. Be ready to perform CPR – see p.172.
6. **Be patient during recovery.** It takes about 48hr to recover.

## Hyponatremia (water intoxication)

Symptoms for hyponatremia are similar to those for heat exhaustion (a mild form of heatstroke); the person will, however, have been drinking plenty of water (but not getting enough salt). There may be cramping in the lower extremities and profuse sweating. If the patient becomes disoriented, combative or irritable, it may have reached advanced stages which, if untreated, can be fatal.

## How to distinguish hyponatremia from heat exhaustion

- **Frequent urination (several times per hour or once every few hours) with clear urine.** Heat-exhausted patients typically pass less urine (once every 6–8 hours), which is a deeper shade of yellow.
- **No thirst.** Heat-exhausted patients are generally thirsty.
- **Haven't eaten much.** Heat-exhausted patients may have recently eaten. Hyponatremic patients may have had a light meal or skipped a meal, but had plenty of water.

## Treating hyponatremia

- **Administer salty foods and water with rehydration mix (see opposite for formula), even if you're not sure of your diagnosis.**
- **Do not give water without rehydration mix.**
- **Avoid commercial sports drinks (Gatorade, Lucozade, etc).** These are low in sodium and high in water and can increase the dilutional imbalance.

# Treating a scorpion sting

1. **Stay calm.** The average adult can survive a scorpion sting with basic field treatment.
2. **Brace for reaction to venom.** The minute amount of toxins injected will likely cause severe but non-life-threatening symptoms for up to three hours. You may experience numbness in the face, muscle twitching, fever, vomiting and restlessness.
3. **Do not apply a tourniquet or cut and suck the wound.**
4. **Take an antihistamine tablet.**
5. **Apply hydrocortisone to the sting area.**
6. **Put a cold or hot pack on the sting area.**

*This chapter was written in consultation with:*

**Josh Bernstein**, *a field instructor and the CEO of Boulder Outdoor Survival School (@ www.boss-inc.com), based in both Boulder, Colorado and Boulder, Utah. The school provided the consultants for the island survival scenes in the movie* Cast Away, *and Josh is the host of the History Channel's* Digging for the Truth.

**Dr David E. Johnson** *(see p.69).*

# Jungle and tropics survival

# Jungle and tropics survival

# Jungle and tropics survival

The word jungle can be used to describe any uncultivated land but in this book we're considering it rainforest, which makes up six percent of the world's terrain. The advice in this chapter can also be broadly applied to the tropics, which extend from 23 degrees north to 23 degrees south of the equator and include savannahs, semi-evergreen seasonal forests, tropical scrub, and freshwater swamps. The jungle and tropics' abundant water and food and warm temperatures (25–35°C, often not below this even at night) make it easier to stay alive if you do get stranded. Because these climates are close to the equator, you can expect nearly twelve hours of daylight year-round with rapid sunsets that necessitate early planning to get shelters and camps prepared before dark.

If nothing else, make sure you bear in mind these basic **rules to live by** in the jungle:

- Keep yourself fully clothed no matter how hot or rainy it gets.
- Sleep off the ground (away from creepy-crawlies and the wet jungle floor).
- Consider insects your primary food source when you need energy, unless you're sure you can identify fruits.
- Watch out for falling debris and don't sleep under dead trees.
- Take good care of your feet; let them get air and dry out several times a day.

# Basic needs

## Collecting water

### From a vine

- **Look for vines with rough bark.** Make a deep notch in the vine as high as you can reach, then cut it off near the ground. Do not cut it near the bottom first, as this will cause the water to run up the vine.
- **Try not to tug on the vine.** This could bring down attached dead wood and injure you.
- **Look at the liquid dripping from the bottom.** If it's a sticky sap or milky, discard immediately (it may be poisonous) and try a different type

# In a jungle emergency

1. **Get yourself and any companions out of harm's way.**
2. **Address any acute medical problems.** See the medical appendix on p.171–186.
3. **Take a deep breath and get your bearings.** Don't underestimate the importance of conquering fear and anxiety. See p.186 to help establish your survival mindset. It's easy to get lost in the jungle, so don't move while you're planning. If recently separated from a group, stay still, make noise (see p.110), and let them find you.
4. **Keep hydrated.** Your need for water is vital in a warm environment. See p.95 for ways to get water and p.89 for dehydration signs and cure.
5. **Make a shelter.** Don't wait until it starts getting dark, make arrangements early. It can get soggy in the tropics (rainforests receive as much as 10m of rain per year), and you want to make sure you're comfortable enough to get ample rest for clear thinking and strength (at least two hours of sleep per night). See p.103 for building shelters and p.105 for fire building.
6. **Plan.** Now that you've dealt with the most pressing issues, read through this entire chapter and cross-referenced sections to prepare more thoroughly for survival. Decide whether you will wait to be rescued or if it will be beneficial to attempt to leave your immediate environment. If in doubt, stay put. Another option for a group is to send one or two pairs of fit volunteers in search of help (in different directions) while the rest of the group remains in place.
   **Reasons to stay put**
   * People are likely to be looking for you.
   * The vehicle you were travelling in or your immediate terrain means that you will be easily spotted from the air.
   * The terrain, weather or injuries will hinder movement.

of vine. If the liquid is clear, let it drip into your mouth or a container to test, but don't put your mouth on the vine, which can cause irritation.

## From plants

* **Look for pitcher plants – those with a reservoir.** Tip them to collect the water.
* **Bamboo plants may have water stored up between the joints.** Look for yellow stems and shake to check for water. Cut a hole at the bottom of each join to access the water.
* **Flowering palms offer a sugary liquid.** Grab a flowering stalk and cut it

- The visibility is poor.
- You don't have a map/GPS equipment and can't work out the way to civilization.
- The sun will soon set.

**If you stay put**
- Set up a signal (see p.110).
- Scavenge for supplies. If there are very few, conserve energy by staying still while you wait for rescuers to spot your signals.
- Improve shelter to increase chances of prolonged sleep.

**Reasons to move**
- The terrain you are in is dangerous (due to flooding, animals, etc) or is exposed to the elements.
- You have navigation equipment and can determine a realistic route to safety.
- It is unlikely that anyone is looking for you.

**If you move**
- Check around to see if there is anything you can take with you that might aid in survival.
- Leave a clue about which direction you're heading in – logs or rocks forming an arrow – in case anyone shows up. As you progress, leave a trail that could be followed, piles of rocks, for example.
- Put something shiny on your pack or hat (such as a CD or aluminium foil) to attract attention of search crews.
- Don't waste time foraging for food (it's not initially important), but do keep an eye out for known, convenient food sources as you go. See p.98 for food gathering.
- Always leave ample time to set up camp each night as the sun will set very quickly.
- Keep a fire going at night when you stop (search crews may search at night with night-vision goggles).

off near the tip; the liquid should begin to flow. Cut off a thin slice every couple of hours to keep it going.

- **Sideswipe dew.** Wake at sunrise, walk through the vegetation and let your shirt or bandana brush up against the dew dripping from the plants. Wring out into a container or your mouth.

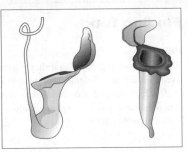

▲ Pitcher plants

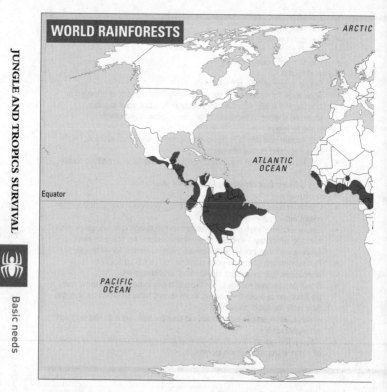

## WORLD RAINFORESTS

ARCTIC

ATLANTIC
OCEAN

Equator

PACIFIC
OCEAN

## Finding food

### Insects

Bugs don't look nice to eat, but they're a survivalist's most reliable energy source (insects are 65–80 percent protein, compared to the 20 percent in beef). There are 1462 recorded species of edible insects; when choosing, avoid caterpillars and spiders as well as all insects that are hairy, brightly coloured or have a pungent odour.

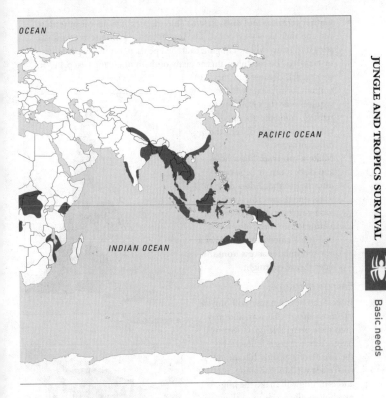

Catching flying insects

1. **Erect a trap.** At night, hang a light-coloured sheet of cloth or plastic from a tree.
2. **Shine your torch (flashlight) onto it to attract the insects.**
3. **Make an insect enchilada.** When enough insects land, fold up the bottom half of the sheet, trap them, and crush them.

Catching crawling insects

• **Look under rocks and rotting trees for grub worms.** They're especially attracted to palms and are perhaps the best survival food in the jungle.

- **Gather termites and ants.** Insert a smooth stick into an ant or termite hill and then slowly extract it. The insects' first reaction is to attack the stick and many will be clinging to it. Scrape them off into a container or bandana. Be careful of ants as many of them bite/sting (see p.113 for treatment). Because fire ants contain formic acid, which requires roasting or boiling to remove, cook all varieties of ants if you cannot discern the different types.

- **Make a can trap.** Dig a hole and place a can or large cup into the ground. Add a drop of water and a few crumbs of any food you have, then cover with a large leaf or piece of wood so that it is shaded but still allows a few centimetres access from the sides. Leave overnight.

### Eating insects

Insects can be eaten raw, will provide the most energy that way, and may even taste preferable (grub worms have a subtle crunch followed by the release of a creamy filling), but if you're not used to it, boiling, roasting and crushing will make the bugs psychologically easier to swallow.

▲ Termite mound

- **Rip off any legs and wings.** Remove the sting of bees and hornets (cut off the tip of both ends if you're unsure). Pop them straight in your mouth or grind them between two stones and eat.

- **Skewer larger bugs such as grasshoppers and hold over fire.**

- **Make soup from insect paste.**

▲ Termite nest

## Plants

Never eat what you don't know or haven't tested properly (see p.197). Clearings and riverbanks, where the sun can penetrate the tree canopy, are usually richest in edible plant life.

- **Look for familiar fruits.** Keep an eye out for bananas, avocados, mangos, figs and papayas.

- **Beware of poisonous lookalikes.** These include strawberry-like fruits (Duchesnia), orange-like fruits (Strychnine) and papaya-like fruits (Pangi).

- **Find any palm tree (preferably a low one).** Lop off the top of the tree to obtain the white palm heart. With an axe or good machete, you can cut down a sizeable palm (one where the first branches are about 2m high). Chop it down about 1m above the jungle floor and remove the outer layers of bark from the trunk. The white core of the trunk is the edible part (eaten raw) and a large tree can provide a mildly tasty feast for nearly 20 people. Palms have something to offer in nearly all varieties from coconuts to dates to a sugary sap.

▲ Duchesnia

▲ Strychnine

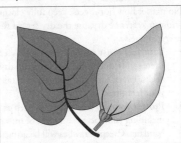

▲ Pangi

- **Climbing a palm tree.** A variation that may help with the climbing technique is to place your feet in a circle of rope (or sarong) as you climb to keep the pressure against the tree, add surface area for extra grip and help you move both feet at once. The rope circle should be small enough so that, when stretched between your feet, your legs are less than shoulder width apart.

▲ Climbing a palm tree

## Fishing and trapping

There's usually ample fishing in tropical environments, but food spoils quickly in this climate and should be eaten immediately. If you see animal tracks you could set a simple trap (see p.190).

- **In slow-moving water, parasites are more prevalent.** Boil fish for 20min or cook directly over a fire until well done.
- **Watch out for crocodiles when fishing on the riverbank.** Keep an obstacle, such as a large log or rock, between you and the water.
- **Be choosy and careful.** Electric eels shouldn't be handled even if dead so avoid all eels unless you can confidently identify them. Catfish have sharp dorsal fins and should be clubbed to death before handling.

## Clothing yourself

No matter how hot it gets, keep fully clothed. If you have two sets of clothing and can keep one dry, use the dry set for sleeping and the other set for everything else.

- **Your feet must come first.** Always clean and dry your feet every night. If there's only one thing you can keep dry for the night, that should be your socks. Every time you take a break, take your boots and socks off to let your feet breathe.
- **Protect yourself from insects.** Keep as much skin covered as possible, including your face; use a piece of mosquito net or cover it partially with a bandana. Creepy-crawlies will be attracted to your sweat and, when hacking through jungle foliage, it's easy to disturb nests of stinging insects.

- **Cover your feet and ankles to protect from snakes, scorpions and leeches.** If you don't have high-top boots, place tree bark, leather, or cloth under or over your trouser legs and tuck into your socks.

## Shelter

### Positioning your shelter
- **Try to camp near a river, but not just beside it.** Look for a high-river mark and camp above it so you're not swept away.
- **Stay away from animal trails and waterholes where you have increased chances of getting a nocturnal visitor.** Look for footprints or droppings if you don't see animals themselves.
- **Do not camp under dead trees that could fall on you.**
- **Sleep off the ground.** This helps keep you dry and away from insects.

### Building a basic bed
**Time:** 15–45min.
**Gear:**
- 4 sharpened sticks or 4 large stones.
- About 6–15 thin logs/sticks slightly longer than your body length (number needed will vary depending on thickness).
- A batch of dense foliage – palm leaves, grasses, etc. Try to find it dry or shake off water.
- Ashes from a fire.

1. **Lay the logs/sticks side by side.**
2. **Hammer sharpened sticks into the ground at the four corners to keep the logs from rolling apart.** Or position rocks at each corner. You could also place the logs/sticks between two trees.
3. **Cover with a thick layer of foliage for padding.**
4. **Keep insects away by sprinkling a ring of ash around your sleeping area.**

## Building an A-frame

An A-frame will put more distance between you and the ground. See p.188 if you need to make your own rope.

**Time:** 45min.

**Gear:**

- 7 2-metre-long sturdy sticks for frame.
- 1–2 tarps and a needle and thread (or dental floss) or about 20 0.5-metre-long sticks for bed support and possibly rain cover.
- A batch of dense foliage – palm leaves, grasses, etc. Try to find it dry or shake off water.
- 5–20m of rope.

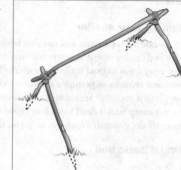

1. **Lash the ends of 2 2-metre sticks together (see p.189).** Separate into an "A" shape.

2. **Make another.**

3. **Set the length of your bed.** Place the second "A" 0.5m longer than your height from the first "A" frame. You may also want to secure one "A" to a tree for extra stability.

4. **Connect the two frames with a stick that sits on the top of each "A" by**

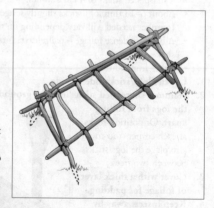

lashing **(see p.189).** This will hold the whole frame in place while you stabilize it.

5. **Carve small notches at the same height on the "A" frames.** Make the notches between knee and waist height, but make sure they are all at the same level.

6. **Use the last 2 2-metre sticks to connect the sides of the "A" frames.** These sticks should be lashed to the spots where you've put the notches.

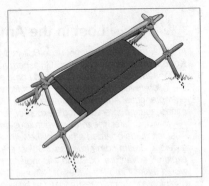

7. **Make your mattress** (using either of two options):
   - Place the 20 0.5-metre sticks across the two sticks you've just attached. Fasten at least some of them so they don't slip off while you're getting on. The rest will be held in place by your body weight. Add foliage to make more comfortable.
   - Wrap your tarp around these same two sticks and sew it to itself with a needle and thread – use dental floss if you have no thread.

8. **Add a rain shield.** If you have an extra tarp, place it over the top cross-beam stick and secure it to the sides. You could also cover the frame with leafy branches.

## Fire

Fire has numerous uses in the tropics. It can dry out your clothes, keep mosquitos away, serve as a rescue signal, provide ash to keep insects at bay and allow you to boil water. See p.199 for fire-starting techniques.

- **Collect tinder.** The best tinder in a jungle comes from standing deadwood since it sheds most of the rainwater. Scrape tinder from the inside. Alternatively, find dry bamboo.
- **Dry off wood with fire.** Once a fire is started, put other damp pieces of wood nearby to help dry them so they can eventually be used.
- **Maintain a safe, controlled fire and always extinguish with dirt before moving on.**

# Lost in the Amazon

*In 1982, three travellers met up in Bolivia: Marcus from Switzerland, Kevin from America, and Yossi Ghinsberg from Israel. They signed on for a tour to a remote village and some gold-mining sites along the Tuichi River in the northeast part of Bolivia. Their guide was an entrepreneurial Austrian expatriate named Karl – a self-proclaimed gold miner, jaguar hunter and jungle expert of sorts.*

A few days later, the three adventurous travellers and their paid Austrian guide boarded a bush plane with some rice and rifles. "It was a lifelong dream come true," said Ghinsberg. "I wanted my 'great white explorer' adventure, gold and wild Indians; Kevin wanted a photo that would make it into the pages of National Geographic; Marcus was pursuing a mystical quest and we all believed Karl was the man to bring all that on."

They trekked for weeks in the upper Amazon basin without ever reaching the promised village or gold-mining sites. Discouraged, they backtracked to their starting point and paid some locals to construct a raft from balsa wood. The new plan was to float leisurely down the Tuichi River to an airfield at Rurrenabaque.

"It took just a few hours to realize we were in bigger trouble on the river. We were completely dysfunctional as a group: Karl was losing his cool because he couldn't swim; Marcus was more miserable as the disease on his feet thrived in the moist conditions; Kevin was frustrated as he thought he should take the lead. I was shaken and torn between them. There was animosity and suspicion and we were speaking different languages so it was a total communication breakdown."

The rapids were demanding and dangerous and, after two days, Karl and Marcus decided not to continue, knowing that even bigger stretches of whitewater lay ahead. Tensions within the group – Karl's bossiness and Marcus's whining – also contributed to their split. They divided the provisions and Karl and Marcus started hiking back upriver towards the outpost while Kevin and Yossi continued on the raft.

The river narrowed into a canyon and the speed and force of the whitewater quadrupled. The boys were launched into the notorious (and unrunnable) San Pedro Canyon.

"The rock was unavoidable; all we could do was throw ourselves on the logs, close our eyes and pray. The clash was deafening. Then we found ourselves on top of the rock hanging above the waterfall. We were locked there under the pressure of the river. When it got dark,

Kevin decided to jump and try to make it to the bank. He made it, but his jump released the raft and launched me over the lip of the waterfall. I was swallowed by the river, into its dark guts. I thought I would burst. It was a long minute before I was spat up to the surface of the raging water. That first breath was pure gold, but hell was just unleashed and the raft and all the equipment was gone."

Yossi managed to recover a small survival kit with some basic first aid, a torch, matches, a poncho and a small amount of food. The young Israeli battled to find his way out of the jungle alone. At night when darkness enveloped the jungle, Yossi imagined a beautiful companion for himself. It helped, but it wasn't enough to fend off a jaguar breathing on his face one night. "I put a lighter to the mosquito repellent and set it afire. The cat's face disappeared behind the big flame, and when the flame died, the jaguar was gone." During his struggle, he discovered his body covered with leeches, slipped and impaled his rectum on a stick, got attacked by termites and developed a fungus on his wet feet that made walking impossible, all the while watching search planes pass overhead, unable to see him or hear his calls. "This was too much to bear, that hope of deliverance shattered was the worst of all. I couldn't take it. I collapsed, face in the mud. I was crying and from the depth of my heart, praying to die."

At one point Yossi sank up to his chest in quicksand: "As far as I was concerned, it was over. I simply couldn't pull myself out and I knew it, so I pulled out Kevin's medical jar and allowed all the pills to fall into my open palm ready to take them and avoid the madness – the mud was above my hips by now – but I just couldn't bring them to my mouth, not after nineteen days of suffering. I jumped headlong into the mud and started swimming."

His quicksand escape paid off; after twenty days sustained primarily by his will, he heard a boat motor, followed by his name. Kevin, accompanied by a local riverman, had found him.

Marcus and Karl were never seen again after the group split up in the jungle. Yossi is now an author and inspirational speaker living in Australia (🕸www.ghinsberg.com). The area where he and Kevin survived gained such international notoriety from Yossi's book Heart of the Amazon that it now supports an expanding ecotourism economy. Even Tico, the local riverman who, together with Kevin, found Yossi, has started a successful jungle tour (and hotel and catering service) based on his fame from Yossi's book.

# Travel

## Navigating in a jungle

- **Move by daylight only.**
- **Avoid swamps.**
- **Use a machete to hack through the jungle foliage.** Chop downward so the foliage falls away from your path. If you don't have a machete use a large stick to knock away heavier vegetation. Bend vegetation backwards as you walk (so the lighter underside of the leaf will be facing you) in case you need to backtrack.
- **Walk around logs – do not climb over them.** It's easy to slip and many will be dead and won't support your weight. Also, you risk stepping on snakes and other hazards out of sight on the other side.
- **Adopt "jungle vision".** Learn to look beyond the trees just in front of you so you can concentrate on the bigger picture and keep going in your intended direction.
- **Use a compass to keep on track.** Dense vegetation blocking your line of sight makes it easy to go in circles.
- **Following a winding river on foot can be difficult.** Building a raft is preferable, provided you always pull over to the edge and investigate any rapids on foot.

For information on **crossing a stream or river** ▶ see p.50.

## Making a river raft

**Time:** 3hr

**Gear:**

- 8–20 3–4-metre-long logs (preferably bamboo or balsa).
- 4 thinner 2-metre-long sticks.
- At least 3m of rope or cord (see p.188 for making rope).

2m

1. **Place two of the thinner sticks on the ground parallel to each other about 2m apart.**
2. **Lay the logs next to each other in a row (on top of the thinner sticks) to form the base of your raft.**
3. **Place the other two thinner sticks on top (just above the two thin sticks on the bottom) and secure them with knots or lashing at the ends to the bottom thin sticks.** This will hold the logs in place.
4. **Test the raft.** If it floats too low in the water, add another raft of the same construction on top of it and secure them together with knots or lashing.
5. **Bring a few leafy branches to help create shade while on the raft.**
6. **Find a pole (one per raft) you can use to steer and move in shallow water.** This will also help fend off debris.
7. **Make or bring something that can be used as an oar.** One per person.
8. **Pick a scout.** If there are several rafts, make sure the lead raft isn't carrying supplies and is manned by enough fit people to serve as lookouts.
9. **A loud roaring and mist are signs you're approaching rapids.** Get to the bank and check it out on foot. You may need to carry the raft around or build a new one on the other side of the rapids. You can also let the raft go down the rapids alone and have people in place to catch it on the other side.

# Hazards

## Freshwater hazards

- **Bilharzia is found in stagnant water.** This parasite can be picked up by just swimming in the water.
- **Crocodiles and alligators lurk at the river's edge.** Be careful when approaching the waterline and do not stay there longer than necessary. On a raft, do not sit on the edge or let your feet hang overboard.
- **Piranhas are not set on attack mode.** They are likely to strike only when there is bleeding or thrashing.

## Land-based hazards

- **Beware of hairy caterpillars.** They are attracted to body warmth and may find their way into your pockets or next to your skin while you are sleeping. Brush them off in the direction they're moving; their hairs can become embedded in your skin and cause irritation.

### Signalling in the jungle

- **Fire and light can't be seen through a thick jungle canopy, and smoke diffuses as it passes though the trees, making it ineffective.** At night, however, it can more easily be spotted between trees by searchers in planes with night-vision goggles.
- **Build a signal fire in a clearing.** If a clearing can't easily be found, try beside a riverbank or on a raft in the river, secured in place with an anchor or a line attached to a tree along the bank.
- **Locate the roots of a "drum tree".** Using a large rock, beat the roots to create a sound that will carry for a long distance. Repeat a pattern of three beats. See p.194 for more on signalling

▲ Drum tree

### Avoiding snake bites

- **Treat all snakes as if they're poisonous** (unless you are confident you can correctly identify the snake).
- **Give snakes plenty of room.** Most can strike at a distance of half their body length.
- **Don't try to get a closer look, pick them up or kill them.**
- **Protect your feet and legs**. Hike wearing long trousers and high boots. If you don't have high-top boots, place tree bark, leather, or cloth under or over your trouser legs and tuck into your socks.
- **Back away slowly.** If cornered, use a large, bushy branch to keep the snake at bay.

# Medical issues

## Treating minor wounds

Even small cuts have a tendency to "go tropical" when you're in high-humidity environments such as a rainforest. Treat even small scrapes seriously. See p.179 for treating minor wounds.

## Removing ticks

Check your body for ticks at least once a day.

1. **Grasp tick as close to the skin as possible.** Use tweezers if available, otherwise fingernails.
2. **Pull steadily.** Adding insect repellent to make it let go may help.

## Removing leeches

If you yank the leech off, put salt on it, spray it with repellent or burn it off, it is more likely to regurgitate into the open wound and cause infection. Most leeches will let go once full (with their blood), but you may not want to wait that long. Try the following method:

1. **Find the small end of the leech.** This is the part doing the damage.

2. **Prepare for removal.** Place your fingernail or blunt end of a knife firmly on your skin just to the side of the small end.
3. **Pry it off.** Gently slide your finger toward the leech and push the small end sideways.
4. **Chuck it.** Once the small end has been dislodged, dispose of the leech immediately.
5. **Clean the wound and cover it.** The wound may continue bleeding for some time, but if you keep it bandaged and dry, and resist scratching, it should soon heal.

## Surviving a snake bite

1. **Brace yourself for swelling.** Take off rings or anything else that might restrict the impending swelling.
2. **Lie down and keep still.** Minimize movement.
3. **Keep the bite site lower than the heart.** This is to minimize the spread of venom.
4. **Get help.** If you're in a group on the move, the bitten person should be carried or remain with a carer or two while the others press on for help. The treatment is antivenin and the faster you can get the patient to it, the better.
5. **Do not use a snake-bite device or cut and suck the wound.** These methods don't work and will harm the person further. Do not apply ice or a cold compress as they will make removing venom more difficult and increase damage.
6. **Wash the bite with soap and water.** However, if you know you may be rescued soon, and were not able to identify the snake, it can be better not to wash the wound so that experts can more easily identify the venom.
7. **If help is on the way, stay still and wait.** If not, try to get carried. If you're alone and still a long way from civilization, make yourself a bed quickly and prepare to sweat it out.
8. **Bandage.** These are not easy to apply correctly, but may provide your only chance with snakes that have potent neurotoxins (not those found in the wild in North America or Europe). Place bandage about 5cm above the bite (in the direction of the heart) to slow the spread of venom. The bandage should slow blood flow, but not cut it off.
9. **Keep the person hydrated.**

## Treating fire-ant stings

1. **Move away from any ants you can see, particularly ant nests, in order to prevent futher bites.**
2. **Brush off or swat any ants still on skin or clothing.**
3. **Take an antihistamine pill or apply hydrocortisone cream to the bite.**
4. **Follow treatment for a minor wound (see p.179).**

# Game reserves

It's not safe to venture into a game reserve without a properly trained professional guide. However, if you should find yourself in an emergency situation, take note of these guidelines:

- **Animals are typically wary of people and view us as predators.** During daylight hours most will go out of their way to avoid getting close to humans. Many dangerous encounters occur as a result of surprising an animal, which can trigger an attack.
- **Walking in open areas provides you with a clear view and allows the animals to see you.** Avoid areas that are too thicketed or dense where you can't see for several hundred metres.
- **Walk downwind so animals can smell you coming.**
- **Alert animals to your presence by making lots of noise: bang a tin cup, whistle or sing.**
- **Don't walk at night when animals are on the hunt.** Sleep in a tree and start walking in the early morning.
- **Each encounter with an animal will be different and unpredictable, although it's worth bearing in mind the nature of each type (as detailed below).** As a general rule, if you find yourself face to face with an animal, do not turn and run – back off slowly, remaining face on and maintaining a somewhat aggressive posture. If in a group, stay together – you'll appear bigger and more intimidating. Don't let anyone run for it.

## Buffalo

Female buffalo congregate in large herds, which are generally seen out on open plains and are quite easy to avoid. It's the older male buffalo (one stray or a group of usually up to six) lurking in the bushes you need to watch out for.

- **Check for fresh droppings and use your nose**. It's possible to smell them when you get near: think farmyard odour. Steer particularly clear of bushes when you see these signs.
- **Look and listen for tick birds which tend to follow buffalo.** These birds make a ratcheting noise while performing a swooping flight.
- **If you do encounter a buffalo and it charges, head up the nearest tree (thorns and all) and wait.** If there's no tree, stand your ground and watch for the horns. The buffalo is likely to dip its head to one side and then swing it upwards. Get flat on the ground so it can't get its horns under you. Either lay on your stomach and cover your head or turn on to your back and move around to keep your feet at the animal. If you get wounded, don't move, play dead and pray it loses interest and wanders off.

## Cheetah

Cheetahs are nervous of almost everything and will move away from you.

## Elephant

Elephants are faster than people and can reach speeds of up to 30kph, so you have little chance of getting away by sprinting over open ground. Even an elephant that's been shot in the head can run another 100m before dropping dead. Male elephants (bigger, solitary and with more rounded heads than females) that are in heat – look for a dark wet patch on the side of their head – tend to be the most likely to charge. But don't underestimate females with calves either.

- **If you find yourself suddenly quite close to an elephant, stop and don't move a muscle. Elephants have poor eyesight and may have trouble spotting you.** Their smell and hearing, however, are excellent. Wait for it to move on, or back off slowly.
- **Watch for a mock charge.** If the animal flares its ears out, stomps and bellows, that's typically a sign of a mock charge and offers a good chance for you to back off slowly. If its ears are tucked back, its head is lowered and it starts moving towards you, that's a real charge and you'll need to take action:
  - **Climb a tree, but only if it has a trunk that is bigger than you can wrap your arms around.** Otherwise, the elephant can push it down.
  - **Head for an area of uneven ground, preferably with fallen trees and boulders.** Elephants can't move quickly over this type of terrain.
  - **As a last resort, lie on the ground and stay as still as possible.**

# Hippo

Don't let the waterlogged-cow appearance fool you: hippos are statistically the most dangerous animals in Africa and can run at speeds of up to 50kph.

## On land

- **Don't get between a hippo and water.** When nervous they flee to water – let them have this escape route as they are likely to move to avoid you.
- **Don't get between an adult and baby.**
- **Avoid grazing hippos.** Hippos wander out of the river at night to graze on the riverbank. If camping close to the river, keep in mind that they can inadvertently step on you because of poor eyesight.
- **If a hippo charges, climb a tree.** If there aren't any, duck or dive behind a solid object or, as a last resort, lie flat on the ground (preferably in a hollow) and hope for the best.

## On water

- **In hippo territory, bang your paddle on the edge of the canoe/kayak every 30 seconds or so.** It announces your arrival so you don't surprise them. A hippo can tip your boat and bite you. The oversized herbivore is likely to take just one aggressive chomp, then leave, but one is enough to be fatal.
- **If you encounter a hippo in shallow water and need to pass by, approach from the shallow-water side so it can flee to deep water.** Sometimes after you have announced your arrival with a knock on the side of the boat, you may notice that that hippo has moved closer when you make your next knock. When you see that this brave/curious hippo is definitely approaching, try to steer towards shallower water.
- **Slap your paddle on the water repeatedly to create noise if the hippo starts getting close and shows no signs of shying away.**

# Hyena

Hyenas are only a problem at night in packs. They can't climb, so you should always try to head up a tree (if you're not already in one) if confronted. If you're on the ground and by a fire or wall, use these to protect your rear as the pack approach and grab a stick to ward them off; do not allow them to circle you and do not run.

## Leopard

Leopards are secretive and prefer to stay hidden away. They are typically not a problem unless wounded, you stumble into their family living quarters, or you surprise them. And you have to be walking very quietly through pretty dense river valleys and thickets to surprise a leopard. Try to avoid rocky outcrops, where they often stay with cubs.

In the open, they'll most commonly move out of your way; however, if a leopard attacks, it will do so from the front (not the back as with most other predators) and will mostly scratch as it runs you over, then makes a run for it. There's not much you can do to help yourself once it decides to attack – it's fast, agile and can climb. Try to protect your face and eyes. If it doesn't hit and run, try to embrace the cat and hold it tight against you while you force your thumbs into its jaws and as far down its throat as possible.

## Lion

Most lions are nervous when people get near and will stay clear, but there are exceptions and lions may follow or even approach you. Always be vigilant for lone males, who may be injured and therefore more aggressive, or females with cubs who will always be more protective.

- **Make yourself look as big as possible (the Masai warriors do this by holding up their blanket behind them, high in the air).**
- **If you're in a group, stay close together and don't let anyone run for it.** Lions attack from behind – don't make it easy for them.
- **Slowly back off while facing the lion.** Move away at an angle and always keep the lion in view so you can see what's going on. Make sure there's not more of them around before you choose which way to head off. Shout your instructions to the group. This makes sure everyone understands what they must do and also helps intimidate the animal.
- **If attacked, fight back.** Punch and grab for their snouts and eyes. Shout and scream.

## Rhino

White rhino stay out in open areas and can be avoided. Black rhino are solitary and should be treated as an adult male buffalo (but be aware that rhinos are faster) – see p.113.

*This chapter was written in consulatation with:*

**Jeff Randall**, *one of the world's pre-eminent jungle survival instructors who runs courses (⊛www.jungletraining.com) in the Peruvian rainforest in conjunction with the Air Force of Peru. He also trains military and NGO personnel and advises film-production crews. He's the co-author of* Adventure Travel in the Third World.

**Dr David E. Johnson** *(see p.69).*

**Joe Charleson**, *who has worked as a safari guide for ten years throughout eastern and southern Africa and conducted walking safaris with the Masai and the Kalahari bushmen. Joe now works with Ker & Downey Safaris and runs Leleshwa Camp in Kenya's Masai Mara (⊛www.eastafricasafariventures.com).*

**Adriaan Louw**, *a senior tracker and evaluator, who has served as chairman for the Field Guides Association of Southern Africa. He trains guides and also teaches a course on dealing with dangerous game (⊛www.fgasa.org.za).*

**Peter Silvester**, *the founding chairman of the Kenya Professional Safari Guide Association. Peter has been guiding in Kenya and Tanzania and has led several members of the British royal family through the bush. He has worked with Abercrombie & Kent, the travel company, and a lion and leopard rehab unit. He now guides with Royal African safaris (⊛www.royalafrican.com).*

Sea survival

# Sea survival

## Basic needs

## Travel

## Hazards

## Medical issues

# Sea survival

**Being stranded at sea can be one of the most severe situations, yet more people die within sight of land than far offshore. Even if you're not planning to spend time at sea, with seventy percent of the earth's surface covered by water, it's hard to travel any considerable distance without crossing a lake, river, sea or ocean. And because it may be inconvenient to grab this book when abandoning ship, it's the one chapter that may be especially useful to read through ahead of time.**

If nothing else, make sure you bear in mind these basic **rules to live by** if you're stranded at sea:

- Don't leave your ship until you absolutely need to.
- Take good care of your life raft. Handle sharp objects with caution.
- Be ready to signal, with multiple techniques.
- Stay out of direct sunlight when hot, and wind when cold.
- Make a sea anchor, tie rafts together and try to stay near the accident site unless land is in sight.

## Basic needs

### Staying afloat without a life jacket

Without the aid of floating debris, even top swimmers can exhaust themselves when trying to keep their head out of the water and stay afloat unaided for long periods. Stay relaxed, let your body float naturally and adjust your breathing accordingly.

- **Float on your back.** Legs and arms outstretched, slightly bent. This is the most relaxing position, but works only in calm water.

# In a sea emergency

1. **Grab what you can.** If your boat is sinking, you may have seconds or minutes to get on the life raft. Start with a life jacket, followed by water, signalling items, fishing gear and clothing. If there's no life raft, look for anything to help with flotation: boards, barrels, water jugs and life jackets.

2. **Radio for help if time allows.** See p.132 for signalling.

3. **Get off the sinking ship if you know it's going down.** But don't be too hasty. Many yachts, for example, have air compartments that will keep the vessel afloat even when waterlogged. If the boat isn't going down, there are no set rules for abandoning. You will be more sheltered from weather, protected from sharks, and easier to spot if you stay with the vessel. You may decide to keep the inflatable raft ready and secured to the boat in the event the boat goes down. Use any delay to collect supplies for the raft and get them ready if you need to abandon ship.

4. **Don't crowd the lifeboat.** Exceeding the limit on a life raft endangers everyone. Once full, others will need to cling to the sides. Urge them to hang on but not climb on. They can rotate with those on board.

5. **Get clear of any sinking wreckage.** Moving upwind is best. Avoid any surface oil or petrol.

6. **Treat any injuries once you're safely in the water and away from the sinking boat.** See pp.171–186.

7. **Have everyone remove shoes and any sharp objects so the raft isn't accidentally punctured.** During temperature changes you may need to adjust the air pressure in the raft. When it gets cold, add more air. When it heats up, remove a bit of air.

8. **Be aware of the weather.** Make shade, put on extra clothes, sit with your back against the wind. See p.126.

9. **Make a convoy.** If there's more than one life raft, tie them together, about 10m apart. A group is easier to spot from a plane. And make a

- **Use survival float technique.** In rougher seas (or if floating on your back is difficult) this will reduce expended energy.

▲ Survival float technique sequence

sea anchor for each boat (see p.134). The boat with the best anchor should be on one end of the convoy.

10. **Keep a flare gun or mirror ready for signalling a passing plane or boat.** Search crews typically look only in daylight hours.

11. **Get organized.** If paper and pen are available, keep track of days, times of sunrise and sunset, when meals are eaten and what is eaten. Also note the names, ages and health of passengers.

12. **Calmly prepare yourself psychologically for survival.** Don't underestimate the importance of conquering fear and anxiety. See p.186 to help establish your survival mindset. Even in this extreme environment, you can take steps to increase your chances of survival.

13. **Plan.** Decide whether you will wait near the crash site or attempt to navigate. If in doubt, stay put.

    **Reasons to stay put**
    - You have sent out a radio distress signal.
    - People will be looking for you (this is likely if you have been caught up in a major storm and people know you are at sea).
    - Wind/currents will take you away from land or shipping lanes.
    - You can't easily steer or propel the raft (if you are simply paddling, for example).

    **Reasons to move**
    - Wind/currents will carry you in the direction of land or a shipping lane.
    - You have the ability to move and direct the raft (sail/motor, etc).
    - No signal has been sent out and no one will be looking for you.
    - You have maps and compasses to calculate your course.
    - You can see land. (If so, try to paddle or sail towards it, or keep tossing out your sea anchor in the direction you want to go and pulling it in.)

14. **Develop a daily plan as you adjust to and learn about the conditions.** For example, stay in the shade during the day, stay hydrated, swim, eat rationed food portion. Write as much of it down as you can.

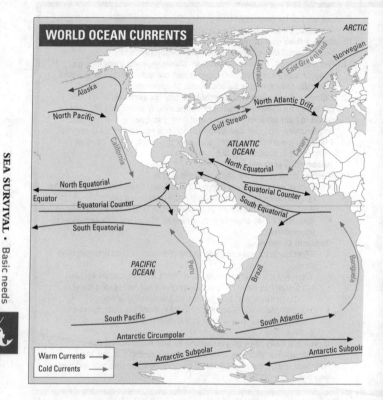

**WORLD OCEAN CURRENTS**

ARCTIC

Norwegian

Labrador

East Greenland

Alaska

North Pacific

North Atlantic Drift

Gulf Stream

ATLANTIC OCEAN

California

Canary

North Equatorial

North Equatorial

Equator

Equatorial Counter

Equatorial Counter

South Equatorial

South Equatorial

South Equatorial

PACIFIC OCEAN

Peru

Brazil

Benguela

South Pacific

South Atlantic

Antarctic Circumpolar

Antarctic Subpolar

Antarctic Subpolar

Warm Currents →
Cold Currents →

- **Trap air in your shirt.** Button/zip up your jacket or shirt and lift up the bottom of the shirt out of the water to trap air, then tuck it into your trousers to secure. If you have a T-shirt, blow under the collar and let the air move to the back so you can float on your front. Refill with a breath or two as the air leaks out.
- **Use trousers to stay afloat.**
  - Tie legs together.
  - Pass overhead to gather air.
  - Hold waist underwater to trap air.
  - Lean on inflated legs.

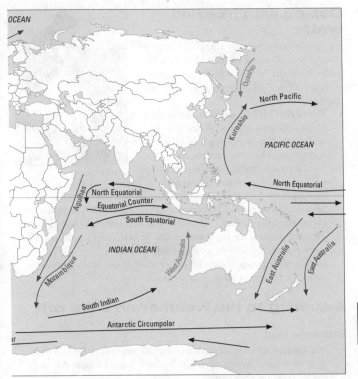

▲ Using trousers to stay afloat

## Coping with freezing water

A strong swimmer has only a 50 percent chance of surviving a 50-metre swim in 10°C water or colder. Keep this in mind if you're considering a short swim to a raft or to rescue someone in the water.

▲ "HELP" position

- **Get in the "HELP" position.** If you are alone and have a flotation device, you can reduce heat loss by crossing your ankles, bringing your knees to your chest and placing your hands high on your chest or neck to keep them warm. Keep your clothing on and it will act somewhat like a wetsuit and cut heat loss.
- **Minimize movement.** Contrary to what you might think, increased heart rate speeds body cooling – cold water takes heat from your body 25 times quicker than air at the same temperature. So swimming around won't warm you up, it will speed up the cooling process.
- **Huddle with group.** If there are two or more people wearing flotation devices, get in a group hug, with chests touching.

## Adjusting to the weather on a life raft

### Excessive heat

- **Stay covered.** Use a bandana or any cloth to cover your head and neck at all times when there is direct sun. Sunburn is an enormous risk; only remove covering when shaded.
- **Try to make shade, either by the way you sit (lying low on the side of the raft that blocks the sun) or by building a canopy.** Take turns blocking the sun if necessary. Make a special effort to do so at midday when the sun is strongest.
- **Take a dip.** Hop in the water and stay in the shade of the raft while you hold on (or secure yourself to the boat with a line). Take the chance to move your legs but keep an eye out for sharks.
- **Wet clothing.** Dip clothing in water periodically to keep cool. But make sure it's dry before nightfall. Even in tropical waters, temperatures can become uncomfortably cold at night.

## Cool temperatures

- **Stay dry and stay covered.** Rig up a spray and wind shield if possible using an extra piece of clothing or canvas and keep the bottom of the raft dry (use a cloth as a sponge – lay it down and wring out periodically). Let those who are strong block the wind and water from those who are weaker.
- **Huddle together.** Sit in a tight circle (think group spoon), everyone holding (massaging) the person in front of them.
- **Dry clothing.** Take off clothes and let the sun dry them the moment the weather allows. If there's no sun, try to dry with wind.
- **Collect seaweed.** When dried, it can be used as bedding and insulation between layers of clothing.

# Drinking water on a life raft

- **Do not drink sea water.**
- **Check for an on-board emergency kit and follow directions for any pills or still included.**
- **Make a still.** See below.
- **Wring sweat out of clothing.** It's not tasty, but it's OK to drink.
- **Collect rainwater.** Be prepared. Don't wait for it to start raining before you have your collecting system ready. Cloth and clothing holds water as well. Wring it out into any containers and use plastic sheets as water holds. Drink yourself full while you can, but at a controlled pace. If you haven't been drinking for a while, rapid intake can make you ill.
- **Melt old sea ice.** The floating mini-bergs that look bluish or grey are old sea ice. The salt content in new ice (which is white in colour) is too high for consumption. Always taste first – a recent storm could provide it with a coating of salt.

## Making a crude solar still

If you have a spare bucket or jar, you may as well try to get a few drops of extra drinking water. This technique will not yield much, but it's better than letting the jar and cloth sit idle.

1. **Put salt water in a jug or bottle.**
2. **Place a cloth over it and let it sit in the sun.** Water will evaporate into the cloth, which can be wrung out directly into your mouth.

# Shipwrecked

*Tami Oldham Ashcraft, 24, and her fiancé Richard Sharp, 36, were experienced sailors – between the two of them, they had logged 80,000km at sea – when they accepted a $10,000 job to transport a private 12-metre yacht from Tahiti to San Diego. They left Tahiti in late September under perfect conditions and spent the first week sailing the luxury yacht in calm seas.*

*When reports of a tropical depression off Central America started streaming through the radio, they decided to play it safe and head north. The storm was reportedly going west, so it seemed like a comfortable margin. But the storm grew and changed direction and they were soon caught in 15-metre seas smack-dab in the middle of Hurricane Raymond with winds of 26kph buffeting the boat. "We would climb up the faces of these huge monsters and become airborne, punching through the cresting top, then crashing down the backside. At times I thought the boat would split apart," said Tami.*

*Richard secured himself to the deck with a lifeline and sent Tami below to ride out the storm in the relative safety of the cabin. Just as Tami settled into her sea hammock, the boat dropped into a deep trough and she heard Richard yell. The boat rolled, then flipped end over end.*

*Tami regained consciousness 27 hours later. She woke up covered in blood, pinned down underneath gear from the boat. Still disoriented, she freed herself and began looking for her fiancé. The lifeline had been severed. She struggled to accept that he had been swept overboard and lost at sea.*

*In addition to the emotional strain from her loss, she was without a mast, engine, radio, emergency signal or any electronic navigational equipment. The boat was partially flooded (barely seaworthy) and much of the food had been destroyed by salt water. She kept the life raft ready, but didn't abandon the sailboat. "I started regaining strength after two days of lying in the life raft,* only crawling out to search for Richard. It was in the life raft that my inner voice first called to me, whispering in my head, 'Get the boat moving, get the boat moving.' At that point it was like a light switch turned on. I went into survival mode determined that I would do anything not to die." She used a sextant to calculate her position. Then she made a small sail and tried to position the sailboat to pick up currents that would carry her to Hawaii, a relatively tiny and easy-to-miss target on the ocean's canvas.

"Eating wasn't a priority for me." Tami said, "I was such an emotional wreck. I pretty much survived on peanut butter on a spoon. Water was an issue and after getting down to my last can of life-raft water I starting tearing the boat apart to get to the water tank and found I had 100l. That was a major turning point."

Tami soon ran out of bandages and medication for her wounds – one of her biggest concerns. With her newfound water supply, she used a drop to clean her injuries, then wrapped them in shreds of ripped T-shirts. She also developed a system to protect herself from the sun while steering the boat. "I shaded myself with a sarong, one side tied to my wide-brimmed hat and the other side tied to my big toe. I allowed myself a little beer as a reward if I made a good day's run."

"At times I wanted to die, just get it over with – why fight so hard to live when Richard wouldn't be there for me in the end? But thoughts of my family and Richard's family, and how devastated they would be not knowing what had happened to us, would slide into my mind and I became strong again."

She continued for 41 days, facing fatigue, injury, squalls, mirages of ships on the horizon, and a near mental breakdown before getting picked up off the coast of the Hawaiian island of Hilo by a Japanese touring vessel.

Tami now lives in Washington State's San Juan islands, where she is a licensed captain of 100-ton vessels. She wrote her full story of survival in the book Red Sky in Mourning.

### Rationing water

You don't know how long you'll need your water supplies to last, so begin rationing immediately. Imbibe the minimal amount to survive and concentrate on regulating your body temperature while you sleep, rest as much as possible and breathe through your nose during the hottest part of the day to keep moisture from escaping through your mouth. The minimum amount to survive is always difficult to calculate and changes with body size, the health of the person and weather conditions. The US Search and Rescue Manual recommends that you drink 0.7l per day in a survival situation, but people have been known to survive on 0.6l (over a couple of months) and others as little as 0.12l per day (over six days).

Do not eat anything but simple sugar if there's not enough water to digest it with. Protein (fish, seaweed) requires the most water; carbohydrates require less. Hard sweets/candies (simple sugar) can actually help by decreasing your water output by as much as 200ml per day by freeing up water in cells.

## Finding food on a life raft

### Fishing

The shade of your raft will attract sea life. Check the on-board emergency kit for any fishing equipment.

- **Catch flying fish.** At night, if you notice flying fish in the area, shine your torch onto a light piece of clothing and the flying fish may fly right into your boat. Club them when they land.
- **Make a fishing kit.** If there are no fishing hooks and line on board, make your own hooks with a safety pin or by carving them out of wood (take care to avoid cutting yourself). Shoelaces can be used for lines.
- **Scavenge for bait.** Use whatever you have for bait. Start with synthetic bait (bits of plastic or cloth), then try small pieces of your food.
- **Protect your hands.** Fishing with the line directly in your hands can be dangerous if you catch a strong fish. Try wrapping the line around a piece of wood or plastic for better grip. Do not tie the line to the raft, as the pull of a strong fish could cause damage, either at the connecting point or where the line chafes the raft. Gloves are also helpful.

#### With a spear or net

Make a spear by fastening your knife to an oar. But also attach a safety line to the knife in case it comes loose. Use a bowline knot (see p.189) through the knife's loop or lash it if possible. You can lure fish to the surface by shining a torch onto the water at night (or mirror to reflect moonlight) or floating a scrap of plastic or a food crumb during the day. You could try using a net, or holding a piece of cloth under the surface of the water, and scooping fish up.

▲ Fishing with a spear

## Preparing and eating the fish

Remember, if you're low on water, eating food can accelerate dehydration. If you catch fish, but have very little water, just chew on the meat, suck the water, and spit it out.

1. **Kill the fish.** Preferably by inserting a knife in the gills and severing the spine. You can also club it with a stick or the end of an oar.
2. **If the fish is unhealthy, throw it back.** If the flesh remains indented after you press it and let go, there's a strong "fishy" odour when you pull it up, and the eyes are dull, consider the fish unfit to eat. Take a taste of the meat. If it's bitter, harsh or salty, spit it out and discard. Also avoid "boxy"-looking fish, armour-plated fish and spiky puffer fish.
3. **Descale it.** Grab the tail and run a knife along the surface against the direction of the scales (back to front) until smooth.
4. **Gut it.** Cut off the head, then cut a line along the belly and use your fingers to remove the guts.
5. **Cut it into strips and let it dry in the sun.**
6. **Eat it.** Take a very, very small bite, then wait an hour or two. If you don't have a noticeable reaction (numb lips, tongue, toes or fingers, itchiness, vomiting or dizziness) take a larger bite and wait another hour. If there's no reaction, continue eating.
7. **Keep the guts and other discarded bits in a container.** Throw it across the wind after checking there are no sharks in the area.

## Signalling at sea

You will be signalling for aircraft and passing boats, only some of which may be looking for you. Search crews typically look only in daylight hours. See p.194 for more on signalling in general.

- **Radio.** Transmitting radios typically have a range of 32km. Wait for a plane or boat sighting before using; otherwise use sparingly to save batteries. The frequencies (typically preset) should be at 121.5MHz or 406MHz, VHF channel 70 or 16. The military frequency is 253MHz.

    **What to say:**   Mayday, mayday, mayday.
    This is [boat's name – repeat 3 times].
    Mayday.
    This is [boat's name].
    My position is [give exact location or landmark or say you don't know].
    I am [lost/injured/adrift at sea, etc].
    I have [number of people in your party, x amount of water left, flares].
    I require immediate assistance.
    Over.

- **Fire flares.** Only fire when there's a plane in sight that's heading towards you. Once a plane is flying away from you, it's too late. Keep the flares/flare-gun dry at all times and take great care when aiming. See p.195 for more on firing flares.

- **Use dye markers if available.** They should be visible for 3hr in calm seas during daylight hours.

- **Make heliograph signals.** Keep shiny metal visible at all times. Use it to direct sunlight towards search craft (see p.194). This is one of the most basic, but one of the most effective, methods of signalling.

- **Splash.** If you're on driftwood, kick your legs to spray white water. Wave any wet cloth around in a circle.

## Catching a bird

If you see birds in the area, lie still and one may land on the raft – wait until it folds its wings before you try to grab it. You may be able to attract birds with a bit of bait on the edge of the boat or in a nest you create from seaweed and whatever else you can find on board. If you have fishing gear, you can place a small hook in the bait. If the bird is hovering but won't land and you have a weighted object on board (a rock or piece of metal) about the size of the bird's head, you might try dipping it in whatever food you have and lobbing it to the bird a few metres overhead. If it catches it in its mouths, the weight could make it lose enough altitude to be plucked from the air. Make sure you throw the rock straight up so you get more than one chance. And take care no one gets hit by it on the way down.

### Seaweed

Look for seaweed, but only eat small amounts of it: it's a laxative and can cause more nutritional loss than gain.

# Travel

## Navigating at sea

Use the sun and stars (see pp.192–193) to navigate. Keep a log estimating your drift speed and which direction you're moving in. Look for clues that you may be close to land:

- **Birds.** Birds typically don't fly more than 150km from shore – heading away from shore in the morning and heading towards shore in the afternoon. A single bird-spotting is not enough of an indication; wait for two or three. Be aware, however, that this is less reliable after a storm when birds can get blown off-course.
- **Silt.** A stream of murky water rich with silt has probably come from a river.

## Maintaining the raft

- **Inflatable rafts.** Keep the raft well inflated, but not rock hard. The one-way valves should not release air when you unscrew the caps but you will be able to inflate by pump or perhaps by blowing. During temperature changes you may need to adjust the air pressure: when it gets cold, add more air, when

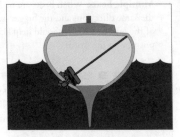

▲ Don't abandon ship as soon as you see water. Try to assess the damage and figure out a way to control the leak. With some creativity, you may be able to find a temporary solution.

it heats up, remove some. Continually check for leaks – look for tiny bubbles coming from parts of the raft that are underwater and a whistling or hissing sound from those above water. Check the raft kit for repair patches or little cones that can be screwed into holes.

- **Keep a lookout.** There should be someone on watch around the clock for leaks, but also planes, waves, sharks, seaweed, etc.

## Making a sea anchor

A sea anchor can keep the boat from drifting too far away from the crash site and also ensure that the front of the boat is pointed upwind and into the waves during rough weather.

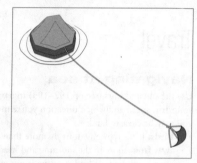

▲ Sea anchor

- **Find and secure anchor.** Find a small bundle of clothes, plastic sack or bucket and affix it with a bowline knot (see p.189) to the front of the raft with a rope.

- **Position the anchor.** Throw the "anchor" into the water and use a piece of cloth to keep the rope from chafing (and potentially damaging) the raft.

- **Multiple boats.** When boats are tied together, they should all be facing the same direction, and the biggest sea anchor should be off the front of the lead boat. This should help keep all the boats in a line in the best position to the storm.

## Making a sail on a raft

Many square or hexagonal life rafts are equipped with ballast bags – sacks fitted beneath the raft that fill with water and help prevent capsizing. These bags make sailing difficult and put you more at the whim of currents (see p.124).

1. **Locate mast.** If there's no mast socket or mast on the raft, prop up a stick or oar by lashing at the bottom or having someone hold it in place. Place clothing or a hard, flat object under it to protect the raft from puncture.

2. **Attach sail.** Secure cloth/ plastic/a jacket to the top of the mast by whatever means available but do not secure to the bottom. Instead, hold the bottom ends with your hands (or attach a rope) and let the sail in or out at the bottom according to wind speed.

3. **If the wind is blowing in the direction you wish to move, get passengers to sit up high in the raft to help catch the wind.** It's a low-power human sail.

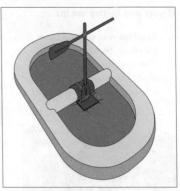

▲ Make a mast

# Hazards

## Fending off sharks

Assume all sharks are dangerous if they're circling your raft or coming at you.

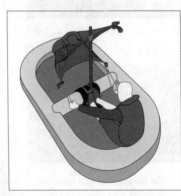

▲ Attach a sail

- **Don't confuse shark fins with fins of dolphins.** With a shark, you'll typically see the dorsal fin and tail fin at the same time. With a dolphin, the back is arched so you're not likely to see the dorsal fin and tail at once. They're also constantly surfacing and diving, and you'll notice the dolphins' breathing blowhole. Dolphins are harmless in deep water.
- **Don't get panicked by whales.** Whales may bump the raft, but will only do so playfully; their slapping tails can be loud and unnerving, but there is very little risk of attack.

### If you are in the water

1. **Bandage wounds and cover jewellery.** Bleeding, shiny objects, urine and faeces will attract sharks, so try to bandage any wounds and cover jewellery.

▲ **2. Watch the shark.** Large circles mean curiosity. Sharp turns and tight circles mean an attack may be imminent.

◀ **3. Bluff aggression.** Swim towards the shark with confident strokes. If it is not deterred, slap the water with the palms of your hands and shout underwater.

▼ **4. Fend off with your feet.** Try to kick or punch the shark's snout. If there are others in the water, form a tight circle with locked arms and feet pointing outwards.

5. **Go for the eyes and gills.** Try to insert your fingers or punch at them.

### In a raft

1. **Stop fishing.** If you see sharks in the area, cut loose any fish you have on the line that you can't land in a few seconds.
2. **Keep hands, feet and sea anchor inside the boat.**

3. **Use a bucket for a toilet.** Keep waste onboard until sharks are gone.
4. **Slap an oar against the water.**
5. **Hit the shark.** Use anything you have if it gets too close.

## Riding out a storm

- **Keep the raft balanced.** Distribute the weight of passengers evenly around the edges of the boat.
- **Lengthen the sea anchor.** If there's more than one raft, lengthen the lines between rafts slightly.
- **Make ready an extra sea anchor.** Just in case the main one breaks.
- **Brace for each wave.** Find a good grip on the boat and keep your head down when the wave hits.
- **Use wind for re-entering boat.** If you fall out, re-enter with the wind at your back. Or wait for a wave to lift you up before pulling yourself into the raft.

## Righting a raft that flips

1. **Find the safety line or sea anchor.** Feel around the edge of the capsized raft, making sweeps with your arm or foot underneath.
2. **Rotate the boat.** You want the spot on the boat where the sea anchor/safety line is attached to be on the upwind side.
3. **Draw the rope across the bottom of the boat (which is currently facing upwards).**
4. **Climb up on the capsized raft.** Use the wind and waves to help you.
5. **Stand on the downwind end.** Pull on the rope until the wind catches and helps flip it.

## Rafting ashore

1. **Try to avoid landing at night or at dusk.** You need daylight (or at least a full moon) to spot hazards.
2. **Select your landing point carefully.** Try to land on the downwind (sheltered) side of an island. Avoid coral reefs and cliffs if possible, which can puncture the rafts and injure you. Look for gaps between the surf for landing spots. If the water hits rocks and creates a high spray, you want to avoid that spot.
3. **Wear shoes and clothes.** Keep your skin covered in case you need protection against rocks and coral.
4. **Surf the smallest wave you can spot.** Paddle to help catch it, and let it carry you to shore. Waves often come in sets; after a set of larger waves has passed, make your move.
5. **Bail out just before the wave brakes.** Dive in and swim down to protect yourself from getting slammed by the wave. Make your way to shore between waves, swimming under any waves that come your way.

# Medical issues

## Treating seasickness

Relentless nausea can reduce your will to survive. When you feel it coming on, act fast. Vomiting can cause rapid dehydration, make others sick and attract sharks to the raft.

### Nausea

1. **Take seasickness pills or use patches.** Follow any instructions on the packet. It's best to use patches or pills before you begin feeling nauseous.
2. **Take ginger.** This works in several forms, such as pills, powder, root or even ginger snaps and ginger ale (if they are made using the real stuff and not a flavouring). For nausea, take 2–4g of fresh root (0.25–1g of powdered root) or 1.5–3ml (30–90 drops) of tincture once daily. To prevent vomiting, take 1g of powdered ginger (0.5tsp) or its equivalent every 4hr as needed, or 2 ginger capsules (1g) 3 times daily. You could also chew a piece of fresh ginger.
3. **Make sure you have enough space and fresh air.**

4. **Concentrate on the horizon.**
5. **Find a task to keep busy, but not below deck.** Check navigation, bail out the lifeboat, etc.
6. **Swim beside the boat.**
7. **Lie down.** Close your eyes. Staring at a fixed object inside will make it worse.

## Vomiting

1. **Wash yourself and the raft immediately.** Removing the smell and sight of the expelled material minimizes the chance of others getting sick and prevents attracting sharks.
2. **GET HYDRATED.** Drink water, don't eat. Use water with electrolyte replacement mix (see p.90 for formula). Start with small sips.
3. **Try to prevent further vomiting (see "Nausea" above).**

# Treating saltwater sores

Prolonged exposure to salt water can cause breaks in the skin that form scabs and pus.

- **Do not open the wound.**
- **Rinse with fresh water if available.**
- **Keep dry, but moist.** Use petroleum jelly or other ointment. It's the process of going from wet to dry that makes things worse.
- **Apply disinfectant if available.**

*This chapter was written in consultation with:*

**Brian Horner**, *president and chief instructor at Learn to Return Training Systems. Brian is a US Air Force survival, escape and evasion specialist, a swift-water rescue technician, scuba instructor, lifeguard, and survival instructor for the US Army and the Department of the Interior. He has also hosted* Split Second, *a National Geographic television programme on survival.*

**Dr David E. Johnson** *(see p.69).*

# Danger zones and trouble spots survival

# Danger zones and trouble spots survival

# Danger zones and trouble spots survival

Travelling in the world's war zones and political trouble spots is common for journalists and aid workers (and adrenalin junkies), and assessing your risk isn't always easy. The stability of some places can vary from one day or week to the next. It can also depend on what logo is on the car you're driving in, how the locals treat foreigners (some may be courteous to press and aid workers in the most violent war zones, others take them as trophies). There are several things you can do to improve your security, from bulletproof body armour for journalists covering the front lines to getting an inner room at an expensive hotel. Start by contacting your embassy upon arrival or before you leave home. Doing so gets you on the list for any evacuation. The most important thing to remember is to stay up to date with the political situation so you're not caught off guard. And have a basic plan in place in case you are.

If nothing else, make sure you bear in mind these basic **rules to live by**:
- Stay informed. Check in with the locals and keep an eye on news reports.
- Have a getaway plan.
- Keep items such as cigarettes, local currency and US dollars for bribes.
- Have an official-looking letter or document stating who you are, and with plenty of signatures and stamps on it.

## In the event of a riot or coup
- **Stay inside.** Follow TV and radio reports and emerge only if necessary.
- **Phone your embassy.** See if they're evacuating their citizens.
- **Get information from aid workers and journalists.** If you don't know where to find them, try one of the town's most expensive hotels which tend to be their gathering places.
- **If you believe the situation will become life-threatening, get out of the country.** As you make your escape, don't draw attention to yourself. If you feel it's just too unsafe to move, stay put and wait a few days for tensions to abate.
- **If a mob is after your car, speed up.** A speeding car is a powerful weapon and people will get out of your way.
- **If you reach a roadblock, have a bribe ready.** (see p.146).

# Kidnappings and hostage situations

Most kidnappers are after money, which means businessmen and high-profile visitors are targets, not rugged-looking budget travellers. Worldwide, Colombia, Mexico, Peru, Brazil, Chechnya, the Philippines and Venezuela are among the kidnap hot spots. According to Robert Young Pelton (see p.148), about 65 percent of those kidnapped get released in exchange for money, 20 percent are rescued, 10 percent are killed and 5 percent escape.

## Prevention for high-risk expatriates in high-risk places

- **Vary your routine.** Alter your route to work and the times at which you arrive and depart.
- **Get a good security system at home and stay alert when entering and exiting.** Leaving for work, right in front of your home, is a typical time and place to get snatched. If you have a chauffeur, make sure they have the car running just outside the front door and can alert you if anything seems suspect.
- **Stay out of the local media.** No interviews, no socialite photos.
- **Hire a professional bodyguard.**
- **Get kidnap insurance.** Several companies offer it, such as: ⊛www .worldwidemedicalplans.com/kidnap.htm or ⊛www.insurecast.com/html/ kidnapransom_insurance.asp. They put up the money the kidnappers demand so you don't have to empty your bank account and sell your home to cover the funds. However, it's worth bearing in mind that the security consultants deployed to deal with the kidnap situation are working directly for the insurance company, so won't necessarily have the kidnapped person's interests at heart. Several companies provide professional assistance in this regard, such as Control Risks (⊛www.crg.com), Kroll (⊛www.krollworldwide.com) and Pinkerton (⊛www.ci-pinkerton.com).

## Surviving a kidnapping/hostage situation

1. **Take a deep breath and flex your muscles while you are being tied up.** When you exhale and relax, the bindings loosen. Even if you can't escape, the bindings will be slightly more comfortable.
2. **Comply with kidnappers' demands without hesitation.**
3. **Speak to captors without anger.** Maintain a relaxed, friendly demeanour. Listen to them, don't chastise them or argue. Rude or challenging behaviour can result in beatings or death.

4. **Strive to keep your mental edge.** Stay focused and alert. See p.186.
6. **Study the captor's features (for description later) and their habits (for possible escape).**

## Dodging gunfire

It's not quite reassuring enough to know that most shooters miss the target most of the time. There are a few things you should do to dodge the bullets.

### Sniper

If you're aware of active snipers in the area, do what you can to avoid going out. If you must go out, take the following precautions:

• **If you're crossing a sniper zone, cross alone.** There's not always safety in numbers. They have a better chance of hitting a group.
• **Sprint in a zigzag.** Use any cover available, such as walls or cars.

### Crossfire

• **Get down and roll or crawl to a safe position.** You can roll faster than crawl.
• **Stay down.** Bullets can penetrate walls, even concrete.
• **Don't take pictures.** Even visibly marked journalists have been shot because their camera was mistaken for a gun.
• **Wave a white handkerchief.** If you find yourself trapped in a street doorway or behind a tree during a small skirmish, wave a white handkerchief. Chances are they'll let you run out of the shooting zone.

## Landmines

There are still landmines in 64 countries that cumulatively kill over 15,000 people a year. Not all areas with landmines are properly marked. Besides the obvious tactic of avoiding areas that are marked with the skull and crossbones symbol, follow these precautions:

• **Don't step off well-used paths when hiking in former war zones.** If you need to use the bathroom and can't wait, keep your feet on the trail.
• **Don't buy "souvenir" landmines or ordnances.** Not only is there no guarantee that they're not still active, their sale encourages kids to risk their lives collecting them for money.

## Passing a bribe

Bribes are not always appropriate. However, if offered subtly, a bribe will rarely make your situation worse. Often the police and border guards indicate that they'd like a bribe – or they may just take one while rifling through your things. If you've been accused of a wrongdoing, this is your chance to apologize, claim innocence, and ask if you would be able to pay an on-the-spot fine to resolve the issue.

- **Don't call a bribe a bribe.** Never offer money directly. It's more commonly going to be called a fine, donation or family gift. You might even make up a term, such as "processing fee".
- **Keep things friendly and the offer will seem more natural.**
- **Goods work as well as cash.** Cigarettes, liquor or a watch or jewellery are among the most common and can feel more like genuine gifts.
- **If there are many officials on hand, find the chief and try to deal exclusively with him.** You don't want to be bribing the entire platoon.
- **Keep cash in different places so they don't see how much you have when you take out your money.**

## Getting around in a combat zone

- **Get a permission slip.** This should come from the most senior ranking military commander in the region you're heading to. The higher the rank, the better. The letter can also be used to prevent checkpoint soldiers from raiding your goods – you can claim that they're for the commander and he'll wonder what happened to them if they don't make it through the checkpoint.
- **Fly your press/NGO logo.** If you're travelling independently, try to catch a ride with one of these vehicles, but don't be surprised if they're reluctant to take you.

## If someone is following you

- **Ascertain whether you're actually being followed.** Take a few random turns to find out.
- **Don't let the person know that you've noticed them.** Look in reflective surfaces so you don't have to turn back to see the pursuers. In a car, check only in the rear or side mirror and do so discreetly.

- **Never head home, down a deserted alley or out into the countryside, even in a car.** Stick to crowded areas.
- **Report them or lose them.** Decide if you want to let them follow you to a police station (if walking, you can duck into any store and ask them to call the police) or if you want to try to lose them.

## Losing someone on foot

- **Get a good look at the person.** Reverse your course and watch for people avoiding your gaze. Be aware that there may be multiple people following you, some ahead and some behind.
- **Head into a restaurant and out of the back door.** Move quickly once you exit as you don't want to be in the back alley with this person if they decide to pursue.
- **Buy a movie ticket, then leave through the emergency exit before they enter the cinema.**
- **Get on a bus or subway, and then jump off from another exit at the last second.**

## Losing someone in a car

- **Get a good look at the pursuers.** Find a dead-end road and then reverse course.
- **Make a turn across traffic at a stoplight.** Wait and then turn just as the light becomes red.
- **Make a sudden exit on a highway.** If you can get them to follow you into a passing lane just before you make your planned exit it will be even more difficult for them to follow.
- **Pull over onto the shoulder of the highway and let them go by.** Do this just before an exit. If they get off, keep going. If they don't, take the exit.
- **If your pursuers are hostile, you could try braking sharply so they smash into the rear of your car.** The rear has no critical parts, the front of their car does.
- **If you lose the car, stay out of sight.** Try a crowded parking lot or garage.

*This chapter has been written in consultation with:*

**Robert Young Pelton**, *who has been captured by death squads in Algeria, held by rebels in the Darien Gap, shot at in Baghdad during countless "airport runs", bombed in Chechnya, attacked by guerrilla groups and has survived a plane crash in Borneo. He has travelled extensively in over 80 countries, including war-torn places, such as Afghanistan and Sudan, and is the author of* The World's Most Dangerous Places, Come Back Alive *and* The Adventurist.

**Paul Rees**, *managing director of Centurion Risk Assessment Services (⊛www.centurion-riskservices.co.uk). Staffed by former members of the British Special Forces, Centurion has provided war-zone training to correspondents from the BBC, CNN, New York Times, Reuters, Associated Press and other major media outlets.*

## Natural disaster survival

# Natural disaster survival

# Natural disaster survival

Some natural disasters can strike at any time, some at any place, but few do both. Therefore, it's worth finding out if hurricanes, tornados or lightning storms occur in the areas you're visiting, and if so, when. If you're heading into a region where earthquakes or forest fires are frequent, you can brush up on what to do in the event that one strikes, or if you're going near the coast, stay alert for early-warning tsunami signs. This chapter can serve only as a guide to what are always very unpredictable situations, but knowing what to expect and what your first steps should be when disaster strikes can help keep you alive.

If nothing else, make sure you bear in mind these basic **rules to live by** in a natural disaster:

- Don't run for the sake of running – stop and think.
- Figure out the safest spot to be and get there.
- Gather essential supplies beforehand if you get a warning.
- Don't use the phone unless it's an emergency.

## Surviving an earthquake

An earthquake typically lasts a few seconds to a minute and ranges from a slight tremor to something that feels more like a wild horse ride. There are more than one million earthquakes each year (about two per minute), or five times that many if you include microquakes picked up by extra-sensitive equipment.

### In a building/house in a developed nation

- **Move to a safe spot.** Get under a sturdy table or crouch next to a solid appliance such as a washing machine. The corners of rooms and soundly constructed doorways may also offer increased safety.
- **Do not rush outside while the building is shaking.** There's a high risk that you'll fall while moving or get hit by debris dropping from above.
- **Avoid windows and fireplaces.**
- **Do not take the lift (elevator).**
- **Do not leave the building until the quake is over.** Be prepared for aftershocks, which may sometimes be severe.
- **Inspect any building before re-entering.** If you leave the building after

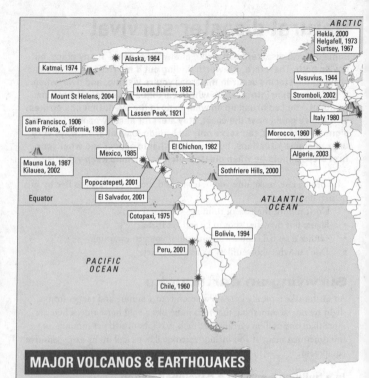

Map labels:

ARCTIC

Hekla, 2000
Helgafell, 1973
Surtsey, 1967

Katmai, 1974

Alaska, 1964

Mount St Helens, 2004

Mount Rainier, 1882

Vesuvius, 1944

Stromboli, 2002

Lassen Peak, 1921

Italy 1980

San Francisco, 1906
Loma Prieta, California, 1989

Morocco, 1960

Mexico, 1985

El Chichon, 1982

Algeria, 2003

Mauna Loa, 1987
Kilauea, 2002

Sothfriere Hills, 2000

Popocatepetl, 2001

El Salvador, 2001

Equator

ATLANTIC
OCEAN

Cotopaxi, 1975

Bolivia, 1994

Peru, 2001

PACIFIC
OCEAN

Chile, 1960

## MAJOR VOLCANOS & EARTHQUAKES

the quake is over, don't re-enter without making a visual inspection for structural damage.

### In a building/house in an undeveloped nation

- **Get out of the building/house immediately.** Without strict building codes and engineering, it's hard to say if the structure will withstand the quake.
- **Move to an open area.** Stay away from buildings, electrical wires and other potential secondary hazards.

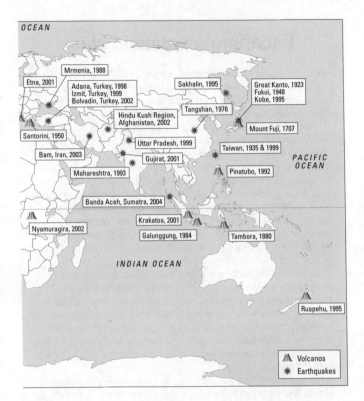

OCEAN

Mrmenia, 1988

Etna, 2001

Adana, Turkey, 1998
Izmit, Turkey, 1999
Bolvadin, Turkey, 2002

Sakhalin, 1995

Great Kanto, 1923
Fukui, 1948
Kobe, 1995

Hindu Kush Region,
Afghanistan, 2002

Tangshan, 1976

Mount Fuji, 1707

Santorini, 1950

Bam, Iran, 2003

Uttar Pradesh, 1999

Taiwan, 1935 & 1999

PACIFIC
OCEAN

Gujirat, 2001

Mahareshtra, 1993

Pinatubo, 1992

Banda Aceh, Sumatra, 2004

Nyamuragira, 2002

Krakatoa, 2001

Galunggung, 1984

Tambora, 1880

INDIAN OCEAN

Ruapehu, 1995

⛰ Volcanos
✳ Earthquakes

### In a car
- **Move quickly to the side of the road and stop driving.** Do not stop under a bridge or beside power lines, lampposts or large signs.
- **Stay in your car.** If stopping near a large object is unavoidable, get down below the car seats, which will help protect you from falling objects.
- **Watch for hazards.** When you begin driving again, keep an eye out for fallen trees, rocks, cracks in the road and unstable bridges.

# Escaping a volcanic blast

*Within minutes of Mount St Helens erupting in 1980, the initial blast had uprooted and flattened every tree to the ground in a 25-kilometre radius. Bruce Nelson, 22, and his girlfriend, Sue Ruff, also 22, were camping with four friends near the old Green River guard station, 23km from where the volcano erupted. Mount St Helens was known to be seismically active at the time, but the group was camping in the designated safe area, known as the Blue Zone. "We weren't any place we weren't supposed to be," said Bruce, who was eating from a bag of marshmallows when he saw the smoke coming. "There was a mountain inbetween us and [Mount St Helens] – which we couldn't even see. When the smoke came, it wasn't like a wall of mass, more like two giant arms billowing down the hill. I remember thinking it looked pretty cool, not scary. I had never seen anything like it. At first, we thought it might be a forest fire. All you could hear was the sound of trees breaking in half."*

*The force of the blast blew Bruce and Sue into a hole left by an uprooted tree. "There was dirt in my mouth," said Nelson, "and I thought maybe the hill had slid over on top of us. I then realized we were underneath a pile of timber that had fallen and created something like a fortress around us. It protected us from the heat blast that followed. My hair was pretty fried, but that's about it." They stayed hidden under the trees to avoid enormous ice chunks raining from the sky.*

*"It cleared and for a few seconds you could see the blue sky and all the damage around. Then came the second cloud – hot white ash, very dense and hard to breathe in. We tied our sweatshirts over our mouths to help breathe and we started crawling uphill, where we thought the air might be more clear, but didn't make it very far because of the fallen trees and zero visibility."*

*They heard two of their friends, Dan Balch and Brian Thomas, call for help. Both were injured. Dan had been pressed to the ground by the initial wind, then covered with icy mud clumps. As he was protecting his head with his arms, the air became superheated and* literally baked the mud to his body, covering his arms with third-degree burns (which he tried to cool in a nearby stream). Brian, who had quickly taken shelter in the alcove of a fallen tree when he saw the smoke, had his shelter knocked aside by other debris and a tree limb had broken his hip. Brian managed to get his hand free and grabbed Dan's foot as he walked by. Dan pulled Brian out from under the tangle of trees – a feat considering the burns on his arms.

They yelled for their friends Terry Crall and Karen Varner, who were both in their tent when the blast hit, but couldn't find them. Bruce and Sue set Brian on the porch of a guard shack, then started walking with Dan, who had no shoes. For the first four hours, hot ash was coming down. They had to walk towards the volcano because the road and river – the main way out – went that direction before turning.

"It was scary," said Bruce. "There were weird smells, the ground was shaking with earthquakes, there were explosions, and we didn't know if another blast was coming. The ash would get pretty deep in places and it was painfully hot even with jeans and hiking boots. We'd sort of run through the deep parts, then climb up on a log to let our legs cool down before we'd continue."

After hiking for half a day, they noticed that in some of the mud puddles the falling ash, which had eased up, was naturally separating and a clear spot could be found in the middle of the puddle. "I took the Cellophane wrapper off my cigarette pack and used that to scoop up the clear water," said Bruce, "It was the only water we managed to get."

They had walked roughly 25km when they saw a helicopter. Bruce recalls the signalling came naturally – it was nothing they sat around trying to figure out. "There was just a few inches of ash on the ground and the sky was pretty clear, so we used our sweatshirts to beat the ground and create an ash cloud, which got the attention of the pilot."

Bruce, Sue, Dan and Brian survived. Their two friends, Terry and Karen, were not as fortunate.

### In a rural area

- **Stay in the open but watch for landslides and falling rocks and trees.**
- **Lie flat on the ground.**
- **A hill can become a landslide.** If on the side of a hill, get to the top if you can do so easily. Or move away from the hill to a flat open space if that is closer.
- **On beaches, move away from coconut trees.** Keep an eye on the sea for signs that a tsunami (see p.164) may be approaching.

### After the quake

- **Put out any small fires if possible.**
- **Use battery-powered torches to inspect your home.** Live flames can be deadly if there are spilled chemicals or a gas leak. For that same reason, don't smoke.
- **Turn off electricity at the mains in buildings where the system appears to be damaged.**
- **Shut off the main gas valve if you smell or suspect a leak.** Otherwise leave it on. If you decide to turn it off, leave it off. Explosions can occur when homeowners improperly turn the gas back on by themselves.
- **Clean up any spilled chemicals.**
- **Be cautious around animals.** An earthquake can affect their behaviour and make otherwise tame household pets aggressive.
- **Prepare for aftershocks.** These feel the same as earthquakes and occur minutes, days, weeks and even months after the quake. They can be almost as severe as the main quake.

## Surviving a volcanic eruption

Stay alert for signs of possible volcanic eruptions when visiting areas known for such activity (see map, p.152). Volcanos always provide advance warning: increased small eruptions, swarms of small earth tremors, increased fume rising from the volcano and sulphuric smells in nearby streams that previously didn't smell. During explosive eruptions, the most lethal phenomenon is the pyroclastic flow, a hurricane blast of super-heated gases, incandescent ash and debris that can travel down a volcano's flank at speeds in excess of 160kph.

- **Evacuate.** If you are in the vicinity of an erupting volcano, evacuate immediately. Pryoclastic flows are typically confined to valleys so head for higher ground if possible.

- **Take cover.** If you are unable to evacuate by vehicle, don't try to outrun the eruption. Look for a strong underground shelter – a cave is ideal. As a last resort, you could submerge yourself in a body of water. You'll need to hold your breath for at least 30 seconds while the hot ash blast roars overhead.
- **Evacuate after the eruption.** Once you've survived the initial blast, continue moving away from the volcano. In low visibility due to falling ash, try to locate a road and follow it (typically heading downhill if you're still close to a volcano). Walk on the edge of the road and use the curb to keep you headed in a straight line.
- **Fend off ash and debris.** Place a damp cloth over your nose and mouth to keep from inhaling the ash. Try to cover your eyes; if you have sunglasses, wrap a scarf above and below them so no ash can enter the eye area. If you have a bike/motorcycle helmet, put it on to help protect from falling debris.
- **Beware of further hazards.** Stay away from rivers and streams that can surge and create mudflows with melted snow, dirt and other debris. Even dry creek beds can become raging rivers in seconds.
- **Move out of the lava's path.** Lava flows generally move too slowly to pose a threat to life. In the case of more rapidly moving flows, remember that they are constrained by the topography. Figure out where a flow is headed (if there's a small valley, for example, that could divert the flow) and avoid its path.

## Surviving a forest fire

If the fire is still small, put it out immediately using a blanket, jacket, dirt or water. Once it's larger, you'll need to take decisive action.

### Fleeing

- **Think, then move.** Do not start running blindly away from the fire.
- **Head upwind of the fire. And stay alert to wind changes.**
- **Do not flee uphill – fire travels fastest upwards.** If uphill is also the direction the wind is coming from, try to find a compromise and run at an angle – moving upwind while not too much uphill.
- **Head for a firebreak.** Although fires can move over roads, dirt fields, ponds and rivers, they do make it more difficult for a fire to continue in that direction.

### If trapped and unable to flee (last-resort options)

- **Find a gap in the fire line.** The fire may be many kilometres wide but not have much depth and in some parts there is likely to be room to run through to the safe, burnt ground on the other side. Place organic fabrics (which don't melt to your skin) closest to your body and dose yourself with water before heading through the fire.
- **Use fire to help.** If you can only go downwind of the fire and see that you will soon be trapped, find or make a small firebreak (a small dirt trench) and set a fire on the downwind side of it. The fire will spread in the direction of the main fire and by the time the main fire arrives, there will hopefully be a burnt stretch of earth to stand on that will protect you.

### After fleeing

- **Use caution and exercise good judgement when re-entering a burnt forest area.** Hazards may still exist, including smouldering patches that can flare up without warning.
- **Avoid damaged or fallen power lines.** Immediately report any damage to electricity lines to authorities. Electric wires may injure people or cause further fires. If possible, remain on the scene to warn others of the hazard until repair crews arrive.
- **Be careful around burnt trees and power poles.** They may have lost stability due to fire damage.
- **Watch for ash pits and mark them for safety.** Ash pits are holes full of hot ashes, created by burnt trees and stumps. You can be seriously burnt by falling into them.

## Surviving a hurricane

Hurricane winds reach speeds of up to 300kph, but the entire swirling system typically moves at speeds of between 15 and 50kph. The storm pushes a tidal surge ahead of it that often floods coastal areas. In the northern hemisphere, the hurricane season runs from June to November, and in the southern hemisphere, November to April.

During hurricane season, stay tuned to media reports. If you have web access, regularly check out storm predictions (⊕www.forecast.mssl.ucl.ac.uk /shadow/tracker/static/tracker_windfields.html). Because hurricanes are large, slow-moving systems, they can be tracked by satellite. Five-day hurricane forecasts are accurate, three-day forecasts more so, but the path is difficult to predict with pinpoint accuracy, so you should prepare for a hurricane if you are anywhere within the projected zone of impact. If you do not have radio or TV news available, signs of an approaching hurricane include fast-rising and dropping barometric pressure and increasing wave swells with abnormally high tides.

- **Decide whether to stay in the area.** When making this decision consider the severity of the hurricane, likelihood of a direct hit, distance from the airport and your access to a good hurricane shelter. If you have the chance to get to an airport and leave (and do not wish to ride out the storm) do so immediately.

- **Locate the best shelter.** If you plan to stay or have no chance to leave, find a strong building away from the coast, on high ground that's not too exposed. This would be a good time to splurge on a nice hotel that has been designed to withstand one. Find a safe place inside, typically an inside room above ground level; a storm surge and inland flooding can put cellar and ground-floor rooms at risk. Call your embassy and get a recommendation if in doubt.

- **Prepare your shelter.** Board up the windows and collect any outdoor furniture or other objects that may become lethal weapons when thrown about by the storm.

- **Locate emergency supplies.** You'll need drinking water (if the local water is potable, fill the bathtub), radio batteries, canned food and first-aid supplies. A camping stove and water filter may come in handy as well.

- **Shut off electricity and gas just before the storm arrives.** Do not turn the gas back on without the help of professionals.

- **Impromptu shelter.** If you can't find a solid building, try looking for a cave. At the very least, get on the downwind side of a sturdy object (a concrete wall), put on any protective clothing you can find (jeans, rain jacket, hat, bike helmet, etc), stay down and cover your head.

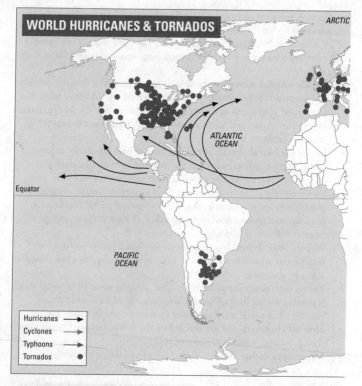

WORLD HURRICANES & TORNADOS

ARCTIC

ATLANTIC OCEAN

Equator

PACIFIC OCEAN

Hurricanes ⟶
Cyclones ⟶
Typhoons ⟶
Tornados ●

## Surviving a tornado

These twisters have destructive swirling winds in excess of 600kph. They are common where hurricanes strike but nearly all of the enormous deadly ones happen across the middle of the US – the flat land between Texas and North Dakota is known as Tornado Alley. The US tornado season runs from March to May in the southern states, April to August in northern states, with about 1200 occurring each year, mostly in the afternoon. You are not, as commonly believed, safe from a tornado near lakes, rivers, cities or hills. But with 90 percent of tornados at Force 2 and below and top winds of 80kph, as tornado expert Josh Wurman says, even in the US "suicide by tornado would be difficult."

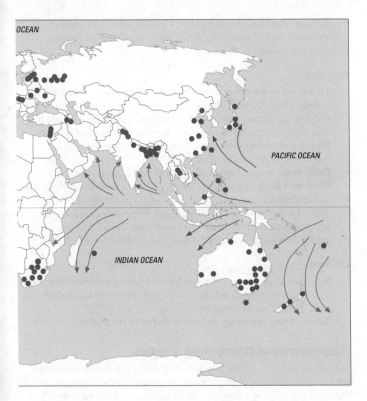

### In a building/house

- **Get to the cellar.** Do not use lifts (elevators). If there is no cellar, get beneath solid furniture on the lowest floor, away from windows. Do not open windows – it's a misconception that this will "equalize pressure". If you can't get to the lowest floor, head to an interior room.
- **Avoid inner doorways.** Doors can be slammed shut by the wind and pressure.

- **Evacuate caravans (motor homes).** These are not reliable shelter from a tornado. Seek an emergency shelter with steel-reinforced concrete, building basement or a cave.

### In a car

- **Do not try to out-drive a tornado.** Even if the tornado you can see is in the distance, there are likely to be about eight to ten in the area, large hail that can take out your windshield and heavy rain that can make it difficult to see the road and leave you stranded in an exposed position.
- **Do not seek shelter under an overpass.** That's where the wind is accelerated and most dangerous.
- **Drive to the nearest house and ask to shelter in their cellar.**
- **Head for a ditch.** A steep and narrow one is best. Bring any useful items (jackets, blankets and helmets, etc) with you to protect against hail and debris. Lie face down and cover your head. If the tornado is upon you and you see an accessible ditch that's narrow and deeper than your car's height, drive in, get down on the floor of the car and cover your head.

### On foot

- **Seek natural shelter.** If a cave or other solid structure is unavailable, take cover in a canyon, ditch or below a solid rock formation. Lie face down to avoid flying debris and large hail.
- **Run to the nearest house and ask to shelter in their cellar.**

## Surviving a lightning strike

Over 90 percent of those struck by lightning are not killed. Moving inside is your best option but isn't a guarantee of not getting hit. You can be shocked indoors if you are using a telephone, electrical appliance, shower, sink or bath. Once inside, stay away from windows and all metal objects.

### When to take cover and leave cover

- **Start moving when you see lightning, start running when you hear it.** Lightning has been known to strike under a clear blue sky, more than 16km from the storm, which is about the distance you can hear thunder. The US National Lightning Safety Institute recommends treating lightning like a snake: "If you see it or hear it, take evasive measures."

- **Wait 30min after hearing the last thunder clap before leaving the safe area.** Don't be fooled by a clear sky. The most common time for an injury or death by lightning is during light rain when there are fewer flashes, typically before or after the storm.

## Shelter
- **Get inside.** The best shelter is a house or building with wires and pipes, which will channel an electrical flash into the ground. Non-grounded shelters are not safe.
- **Get into a vehicle with a metal roof.** This is better than being in the open or in a shelter not grounded by wires and pipes. Tyres are insulating but lightning can spark 3–6m, so a vehicle is not completely safe. You've got the same risk of getting hit if you're moving or parked, so head for more protection such as under a bridge or overpass.
- **Seek shelter in a cave.** Do not sit or stand against the rock on either side or at the back or entrance of the cave – stay a metre away. Do not venture far into any cave and beware of old mines with metal beams.

### Without shelter

- **Move away from flat, open terrain, high ground, water, metal objects, rocky outcroppings and solitary tall trees.**
- **Head towards ditches, low ground or clumps of shrubs or trees of the same height.**
- **Groups should scatter 5–7m apart.** That way, those not hit by lightning can help others.
- **Crouch down.** Place feet together. If you have a foam pad or piece of rubber with you, place it under your feet. Do not lie down, which exposes your heart to dangerous ground currents. You may wish to put your hands over your ears to minimize the thunder's acoustic shock.

### On the water

- **Get to shore if you are close and can get good cover or shelter.**
- **Tall trees and rocky outcrops on shore may be more dangerous than staying on the water.** If your boat has a cabin, getting inside and staying away from all metal objects may be a safer bet.
- **Stay low in an open boat.** In a canoe, row boat or small sailboat, lie down (preferably on top of an extra life jacket) and make sure you're not in contact with metal objects.

For information on **surviving a sandstorm** ▶ see p.87, for **surviving an avalanche** ▶ see p.62.

## Surviving a tsunami

These giant, fast-moving sea surges, caused by an earthquake or volcanic eruption out at sea, can create waves of up to 45m that move at speeds of up to 50kph when they hit shore. They often arrive with very little warning, striking the coast and inundating low-lying areas more than a kilometre inland. The Pacific Ocean is the most seismically active (the US and Japan monitor these waters but many countries don't have the infrastructure to disseminate emergency warnings). Countries around the Indian Ocean are working to put tsunami warning systems in place (much of Thailand had already done so at the time of writing) but it is likely to be several years before this is fully operational. Risk of tsunamis is significant in the Caribbean and low in the Mediterranean.

- **Pay attention to earthquakes.** If you feel a tremor while staying near the coast, be aware that you may not be at the epicentre of the quake. A stronger quake could have occurred out at sea that has started conditions for a tsunami. Try to get immediate reports about where the epicentre was. If you can't, move to higher ground or keep an eye on warning signs (see below).
- **Look for danger signs.** The first thing you may notice at the shore is that the water suddenly and dramatically recedes, leaving shallow-docked boats on land and fish flopping about. Other signs include a loud, sustained roar and shaking ground. In this instance you are likely to have only several minutes to run from the beach and uphill if possible. Even if the wave may not look like much while it's still far out to sea, evacuate immediately. An earlier but less accurate sign is animal behaviour. Many are more sensitive to ground tremors and may behave strangely or flee inland.

## On land

- **Move to high ground or a solid, tall building.** If you can't get that far away or can't find high ground quickly, look for a solid multi-storey building and get as high up as possible, preferably to the roof where you can be rescued by helicopter (see p.194 for signalling).
- **Do not grab onto something low or climb into a vehicle for safety.** If you do manage to grab a tall lamppost or similar structure, lock your arms around it, but don't hug the object tightly; you want to rise up to the surface with the water level. Look around at all times, as you may have to dodge large objects floating by.
- **Don't return to the shore after the first wave has receded.** Tsunamis can consist of a series of waves, the heights of which may vary significantly.

## If in a boat

- **If you can't make it to shore and get to high ground in time, head further out to sea.** In deeper water (the deeper the better) the waves are typically not as large or dangerous.

*This chapter was written in consultation with:*

**Bill McGuire**, *Benfield Professor of Geohazards and Director of the Benfield Hazard Research Centre, Europe's largest, multidisciplinary academic hazard research centre. Bill is a TV commentator on disasters, a science writer, Fellow of the Royal Institution, Chief Consultant for the BBC science drama,* Supervolcano, *and author of several books including* A Guide to the End of the World: Everything you Never Wanted to Know.

**Richard Kithil Jr**, *founder of the National Lightning Safety Institute (®www.lightningsafety.com).*

**Tim Baker**, *Tornado Chasing School instructor (®www.tornadochaser.net).*

## Coping after a disaster has passed

- **Leave (and help others to leave) any areas that are unsafe.** Check for gas leaks, live electrical wires and chemical spills.
- **Treat any medical emergencies** (see pp.171–186).
- **Use a phone only in emergencies such as fire, medical problems and looting.** The communication system will probably be already overburdened. Listen to a radio or watch TV to gain information on the situation and send a text message (SMS) home to inform friends and family of your status.
- **Locate your food and water supplies and ration.** If the water supply is low, start minimizing consumption and use.
- **Leave quickly or risk having to stay for several days.** Get to your embassy, the local airport or the nearest international airport as quickly as possible. Routes may be blocked by disaster damage; in which case notify your embassy and seek their advice.

### If you want to stay

Your volunteer services may be appreciated, especially in the short term, but understand that you will also be drawing on the local resources – water, food, blankets and other supplies that are badly needed by the locals. Also, consider the risks: disease outbreaks in underdeveloped nations are more common after natural disasters. If you have even minor wounds, they can become seriously infected, especially in tropical areas, and you're likely to receive less help from medical services that are already overstretched. If you do decide to stay, consider the following:

- **Try to secure supplies: adequate clothing, food, blankets and a torch (flashlight).**
- **Be meticulous about getting clean water.** If bottled water cannot be found, try water purification tablets, iodine, a filter, boiling (for about 10min), catching rainwater or distilling (see p.201). You'll need at least 2l per person per day (more in hot climates) and it should be stored in cool, dark places so algae doesn't form. See p.130 for rationing in extreme situations.
- **Maintain the highest levels of hygiene possible.** Wash often, especially after using the toilet. Wash with sand when no water is available and do not put your fingers in your mouth or bite your nails. Keep clothes (especially underwear) washed if you can do so without using valuable drinking water.
- **Wear a mask.** Try to get one issued from first-aid personnel. There may be harmful contaminates in the air, such as asbestos from buildings that have come down. Wear a bandana if no mask is available.

**Appendices**

# Appendices

# 1: Field medicine

Before administering any first aid, always make sure that you're not putting yourself in danger. You (or any professional rescuers) may need to move someone away from danger quickly before administering care. All the procedures in this appendix apply only to adults. If you have medical gloves available, use them whenever treating wounds.

## Unconscious person

1. **Check if the person is conscious.** Do this by firmly rubbing your knuckles on their chest plate (sternum) and loudly calling, "Are you awake!?" If there's no response, send someone to get medical assistance while you proceed to step 2.

2. **Put the person on their back.** In cases where someone has fallen more than three times their height or been in a car accident, assume they may have a spinal injury and do not move them if professional medics are available. If they are not available, you'll need to turn the person very carefully with a group. The person should be rotated with a "log roll" – the entire body at the same time – with as much support as possible.

3. **Use a jaw thrust to open the airway.** Kneel behind the person's head, place your fingers behind the angle of the jaw and your thumbs on either side of the chin (with the padded base of your thumbs resting on their cheeks) and then lift the jaw gently upward with your fingers. If there's a neck injury, this method is safer than simply tilting their head back but if you can't manage to get the airway open with the jaw thrust, tilt their head back anyway. The airway takes precedence.

4. **Check to see that the airway is not blocked by an object in the mouth.** If it is, use a finger to remove it.

5. **Keeping the head in position with chin tilted back, put your ear to their mouth and listen for breathing sounds.** Also, look at the chest and neck for any signs of movement that indicate breathing. Do this for 10 seconds (20 seconds if the person is very cold). If the person is breathing, place them in the recovery position (see p.173).

6. **Pinch the nose shut and hold it while the chin is still tilted backward.** Seal your lips over the person's mouth and exhale gently into their lungs. If the chest rises, the airway is clear. If not, check that the chin is tilted back enough and open their mouth and check again for obstructions.

7. **Blow in two full breaths, then check for breathing, coughing, movement or other signs of circulation.** Use a capillary refill test to check for circulation: press down on a finger- or toenail. The skin beneath the nail should go white and then back to pink within 3–4 seconds of release. Other signs of a lack of circulation include lifelessness, cold and clammy skin, and a bluish colour in the face and lips. If you get a pulse but no breathing, continue giving one breath every 6 seconds until the person resumes breathing.

8. **If there is no circulation and you suspect that the person has had a heart attack (you saw them collapse holding their chest), deliver two hard thumps to the chest with the underside of your fist.** This precordial thump can help jump-start the heart but can also crack the ribcage. If you did not witness them collapse, go directly to step 9.

9. **Begin chest compressions.** Move to the person's side and find the sternum, which is the bone between the ribs in the centre of the chest.

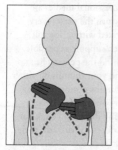

Locate the soft notch just below the sternum. Place the heel of your hand two fingers' distance above it. Place your other hand on top, interlock your fingers and press downwards quickly, using your weight to help depress the chest. Press about 4cm down at a rate of 100 per minute. Administer fifteen such compressions, followed by two breaths, followed by fifteen more compressions. Don't stop to check for a pulse – keep going until you notice any signs of life.

▲ Locate sternum

10. **Repeat the breathing and compressions until help arrives.** If you started administering Cardio Pulmonary Resuscitation (CPR) within a few minutes of the person's heart stopping (or even longer if the person was in very cold conditions or is intoxicated), keep up the CPR as long as possible. Under normal conditions, brain damage can start to occur after the person has not been breathing or had circulation for 3–5min.

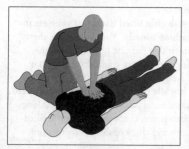

▲ Compressions

## Recovery position for unconscious person who is breathing

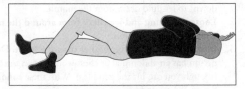

- Keep the person's head turned to one side so the airway remains open in case of vomiting.

- Keep the person out of sun and wind and try to ensure they are at a comfortable temperature.

- Do not try to force-feed them food or fluids.

- Do not elevate feet.

- Check circulation (using the

capillary refill test – see opposite) in the lower arm every 10min. If you don't see signs of circulation, but they're still breathing, treat for shock (there may be internal bleeding causing a loss of blood pressure). If circulation and breathing stop, initiate CPR.

## Treating for shock when someone is conscious

Shock usually occurs within the first hour after a major injury. Signs include: pale or bluish skin that's cold to the touch or clammy from sweating, restlessness, thirst, confusion, nausea, vomiting, grey skin and fainting. The severity depends on the type of injury, amount of blood lost and characteristics of the injured person's nervous system. Pain, rough handling, delayed treatment of the injury, fear and panic can all make shock more severe. Untreated, shock can become life threatening.

1. **Put the person on their back on level ground.** If breathing is difficult, have them sit up (semi-reclined) with knees raised and feet down – a "W" position. If the person is vomiting, lie them on their side (injured side down) to let fluid drain from the mouth.
2. **Loosen clothing and jewellery from around the neck and waist to allow better circulation.**
3. **Elevate the person's feet higher than the heart.** Do not do this if the person has an abdominal or chest wound or an unsplinted leg fracture (though you can lift the good leg). With these conditions leave the feet flat on the ground.
4. **Maintain the person's body temperature.** Do what you can to prevent chills and overheating with whatever is available: blankets, body heat, cool-water compresses, fanning, etc. Make a shelter to protect them from sun and wind and insulate them from the ground with leaves and dry grass.
5. **Reassure the person that they're OK and not alone.**
6. **Give only tiny amounts of fluid at room temperature every 15min if you're more than 2hr from help.** Add an eighth of a teaspoon of salt, if available, to each half glass of fluid. If you're likely to get assistance within 2hr do not give them anything. In cases where surgery is necessary it is better if the person has not drunk anything. Do not give the person any food.

## Saving someone from choking

A person who is choking cannot talk, cough or breathe, and may turn red or blue in the face. Do not begin a rescue procedure until you are sure they are choking.

1. **Ask "are you choking?" and look for head nod or other affirmative sign.**
2. **Encourage them to cough hard.**
3. **Slap them between the shoulder blades five times while you hold onto them with your other hand.**
4. **Perform the Heimlich manoeuvre up to five times while someone else calls for help (if possible).** Stand behind them and press your fist (thumb inward) into the person's stomach, just below the ribcage. Grab the fist with your other hand and pull inwards and up sharply.
5. **Repeat the procedure (five back slaps, five Heimlich manoeuvres) until blockage is cleared or the person passes out.**
6. **If the person passes out, lay them face up and check that their mouth**

**is clear of any coughed-up objects.** Look closely as you try to remove any obstruction by reaching deep into their mouth with two hooked fingers. If you do this without looking you risk pushing any coughed-up object back down their throat.

7. **Blow the object in.** Tilt their head back, pinch their nose and blow. Try this up to five times. Then do fifteen chest compressions (regardless of state of the heart). Repeat until object enters the lung and they resume breathing or professional help arrives.

## Carrying an injured or unwell person

**Conscious person**

**Unconscious person**

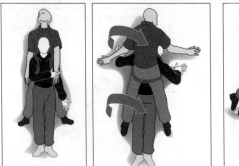

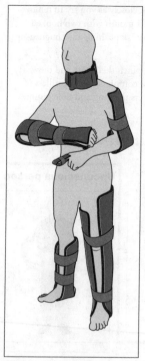

▲ Splints

# Treating an arm or leg fracture

## Determining if there's a fracture

There's not always a loud breaking sound and a limb bent the wrong way.

**1. Look for swelling and discolouration.** If this appears in a spot where there's no joint, it's an especially strong indication of a fracture. If you can wiggle your fingers or toes, the limb may still be broken.

**2. Feel for a ridge – gently.** If there's a break you can often feel a ridge in the place where it's most sore.

**3. Gently straighten the injured limb as**

▲ Making a sling, step 1

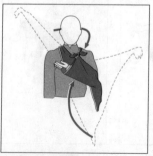

▲ Making a sling, step 2

▲ Making a sling, step 3

much as possible (without forcing it) and press the whole limb in the direction of your torso. This can be as simple as straightening your leg and standing on it with some of your weight or holding your arm straight and parallel to the ground and leaning against a tree. If it hurts when you do this, it's likely to be broken.

4. **Check the fingers or toes in the injured limb for circulation.** See below for how to do this.

## Waiting for help

If you can get help within 7 days:

- **Immobilize the fracture and wait for help.** To keep the fractured limb from moving, secure it with pliable metal splints if available (see opposite). You can also improvise with sticks, the metal bars in an internal-frame backpack, tape, bandages and bandanas. With arm fractures, a sling (triangular bandage that holds the arm in front of you and is tied around the neck; see opposite) is a smart addition to an arm splint, but can be effective on its own as well.

## Resetting a fracture

You should try to reset the fracture only if one of these three criteria is met:

- **There's no circulation to the fingertips or toes of that limb.** To check for circulation in the hand or foot of the damaged limb, use a capillary refill test (see p.172). Also check if the fingers or toes in that limb are cold and turning purple or grey. If the limb is not getting circulation it's because a fracture is pinching a vessel and cutting off blood supply. You must take action to reset the bone. If you don't, the limb will die in about 6hr if you can't get help in that time.

- **You're quite sure you won't get medical attention for 7 days.** If you're not sure, you may wish to wait a few days just in case. It takes a week before an unset broken limb will start healing incorrectly.

- **It's too difficult to evacuate the person without resetting.** If a limb is broken in such a way that, for example, the person can't lie down on a stretcher.

### Procedure

1. **Construct traction device.** This is a brace that helps stretch the muscles to their normal length, reduces pressure on the bone, keeps blood flowing, controls muscle spasms and allows the limb to heal correctly. A

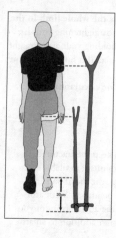

professional traction splint is ideal for expeditions (Hare Splint or Kendrick Traction Device), but is cumbersome for individual travellers.

**2. Pull on the limb.** You'll need to pull to separate the overlapping bones. This can typically be done by having someone pull on the limb (often a few minutes is required if done immediately, otherwise 5–10min or more if you've waited more than 10min after the injury). With an arm injury, you can also hang with your bad arm from a branch or pole, or stand with the bicep of your good arm wrapped around a pole or the trunk of a small tree while someone pulls on the hand of the broken arm so that it's parallel to the ground. Often, you won't feel it click back into place, but you will probably notice the ridge or odd angle is gone.

**3. Traction into position.** Secure the traction device. By twisting the cord connecting the foot to the bottom of the traction device, tension can be applied to the limb.

**4. Splint into stable position.** Secure limb and minimize movement.

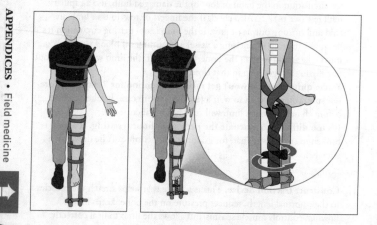

## Stopping a bleed

1.  **Remove any clothing and blood to find the source of the bleeding.**
2.  **Place your hand over the wound and apply firm pressure if no bandage or cloth is immediately available.**
3.  **Raise (if possible) that body part above heart level.** If you suspect a fracture on that body part, do not raise it.
4.  **Wrap it.** Wind a band of cloth (elastic bandage, bandana, T-shirt) around the limb while slowly removing your hand. Place a small solid object such as a smooth stone or stick just over the site of the wound and continue wrapping the bandage. The object helps put pressure on the wound to stop the bleeding. This bandage can be held in place by hand or with any tape you have available. It should be tight enough to stop the bleeding but not cut off circulation.
5.  **Don't peek at the wound.** Keep the pressure constant for 15min. If it bleeds through whatever you're using as a bandage, don't replace it, just add more cloth or material on top and maintain pressure.

## Cleaning and preparing a wound

1.  **Remove any large pieces of dirt or other debris from the wound with tweezers.**
2.  **Wash the wound gently under running water.**
3.  **Add soap and continue washing.** Gently scrub the wound until clean with cloth or gauze if available.
4.  **Sterilize with iodine, medical sterilizer or urine.** If you have a water bottle, you can also squirt to rinse the wound after adding about a dozen drops of iodine or other medical sterilizer to it. If neither of these options is available, use urine as a last resort. If it comes directly from the source and is directed at the wound, it is a sterile fluid that won't introduce infection.
5.  **Let the surrounding skin dry.** Pat dry with a sterile bandage or gauze if available.
6.  **Cover with a bandage but leave the wound open.** Do not sew it closed or seal it shut with tape or glue. (However, for a gaping wound, tape or a butterfly bandage pulled across the edges can help keep it from tearing more.) In the wilderness, some infection is likely and the wound should be allowed to drain. See below for infected wounds.
7.  **Change the dressing daily.**

### Treating road-rash scrapes

Cover with a dry gauze pad and tape around the perimeter. When removing the dressing, water will help loosen any bandages sticking to the wound.

## Treating an infected wound

Signs of an infection include: swelling, pus, redness and increased temperature around the wound, and pain.

1. **See a doctor (if possible) about taking a course of antibiotics.**
2. **Apply a warm compress directly on the wound for 30min.** Repeat three times daily.
3. **Puncture and drain the wound with a sterile probe.** A needle sterilized by a flame or iodine works well. Poke the wound gently in several places, then gently press on the edges to drain pus.
4. **Keep the wound open but covered with a bandage.**

### Maggot therapy for wilderness situations

1. **Remove the bandage and expose the wound to flies for 24hr.**
2. **Cover the wound.** Maggots will develop and begin cleaning dead tissue from the wound.
3. **Remove the maggots once they've eaten all of the dead tissue.** Use sterile water and antiseptic to wash them away before they begin eating healthy tissue.
4. **Cover with a clean bandage.** Monitor the wound several times daily to make sure all maggots are gone. The wound should heal normally.

## Burns

1. **Treat for shock.** See p.173.
2. **Remove clothing and jewellery from the burnt area.** Do not do this if it is stuck to the skin.
3. **Pour cool water gently over the burnt area.** Do this for at least 10min, 20min for chemical burns. Do not use water that may be contaminated.
4. **Do not use soap, apply creams or pop blisters.**
5. **Wrap the burnt area with dry bandages (non-stick if available).**
6. **Seek medical help.**

# Diagnosing and treating malaria

No prophylactic drug makes you 100 percent safe. If you are taking them or other precautions (such as spraying with DEET mosquito spray, wearing long clothing and using mosquito coils and a mosquito net) and get sick while travelling in an area where malaria is prevalent, you should be alert to the symptoms and take the relevant action.

### Determining if you have malaria

- **Look for the following symptoms:** chills and fever lasting several hours and occurring every 3 or 4 days, often accompanied by headache, jaundice (yellowing skin) and muscle and joint pains.
- **Get tested.** It's not possible to determine with certainty without a doctor's test, so seek medical attention if you suspect you may have malaria.

### Treating malaria when you can't get to a doctor

Lariam (mefloquine) tablets can be taken in an emergency dose. Take 3 tablets, then 1 tablet after 6–8hr.

# Treating sprains and strains

Sprains and strains can be treated in the same way (it's unlikely you'll be able to diagnose one from the other).

1. **Lie down and elevate the sprained/strained area immediately.** Do this within seconds.
2. **Wrap the affected area immediately and apply ice if available.** An elastic bandage is ideal but your shirt will work and also save time. Place ice over the bandage so it is not in direct contact with the skin. Ice should be applied for 15min and then removed for 40min, and this cycle should be repeated for the first 24hr.
3. **Re-wrap more loosely if the swelling causes the bandage to feel constrictive.**
4. **Rest it.** If you can refrain from using the body part, try to do so. If you absolutely must move on, limp and use a walking stick or arm sling to minimize damage to the injury. Keep it elevated when not using to avoid swelling.

# Treating an eye infection

Symptoms of an eye infection include swelling of eyelash follicles and soreness. Treat with frequent water compresses (a cloth soaked in water). If available, rub chloramphenicol cream into the eyelids.

# Treating urinary tract infections

1. **Look for the following symptoms:** discomfort when passing urine, cloudy and offensive smelling urine, increased frequency when passing urine, loin pain, shivers and fever.
2. **Get to a doctor if possible.**
3. **In the wilderness treat with ciprofloxacin.** We do not recommend taking prescription medication unless it has been prescribed specifically for you. However, in an emergency situation you may feel there is no alternative, in which case take 250mg twice daily for 3 days.

# Dysentery

## Treating when near a city or town

If you can get to a city or town with a medical clinic, do so. Even undeveloped countries have these in every town.

1. **Drink large amounts of water to avoid dehydration.** If you have a rehydration mix in your first-aid kit, add it to any water you consume. See p.90 for making your own.
2. **Get to a medical clinic and leave a stool sample.** Do not "ride it out" by waiting to see if it might cure itself, especially if you have fever or see blood in your stools. Nor should you take an anti-diarrhoea pill (Imodium) before a diagnosis is made. If you must remain near a toilet, put a stool sample in a film canister and have a friend or fellow traveller take it to the clinic.
3. **Keep taking fluids and introduce food slowly.** Rice, white bread, banana and boiled vegetables are good for starters.

## On the move

Carry an Imodium pill in your money belt in case dysentery strikes on a bus or at other times when you're not prepared to handle it and don't have your first-aid kit to hand. Address the problem thoroughly as soon as you're able to get to a city or town.

## If in a remote area and can't get to a medical clinic

Try to make a self-diagnosis if you have the drugs to treat it (see opposite).

| | Blood in stool | Fever | Incubation period | Duration | Other symptoms | Treatment |
|---|---|---|---|---|---|---|
| Food poisoning | No | No | 2–6hr | 5–8hr | Sudden onset, often with vomiting | Drink fluids |
| Giardia (Amoebic Dysentery) | No | No | 2–6 weeks | Ongoing, requires treatment | Offensive stools and flatulus | Metronidazole (2g daily for 3 days), followed by furamide (500mg every 8hr for 10 days) |
| Travellers' Diarrhoea | No | No | 12–48hr | 2–5 days | Chills, abdominal cramps | Ciprofloxacin (250mg*) |
| Salmonella | Yes | Yes | 12–72hr | 4–7 days | Headache, nausea stomach pain | Ciprofloxacin (250mg twice daily for 3 days) |
| Shigella | Yes | Yes | 6–24hr | 2–5 days | Nausea, vomiting | Ciprofloxacin (250mg twice daily for 3 days) |
| Campylobacter | Yes | Yes | 2–5 days | 2–5 days | Severe stomach cramps, nausea, vomiting | Erythromycin (500mg 4 times daily for 5 days) |

* Typically, 2 x 250mg pills will do the trick, but not taking a full course of the antibiotic can create strain-resistant viruses that can cause far greater danger to all humans at a later stage and is therefore not recommended. This is a "heavy artillery" drug for basic dysentery (many doctors would start treatment with a milder drug that is often effective) and if you do not make the right diagnosis, Ciprofloxacin can upset your intestinal lining.

We do not recommend taking prescription medication unless it has been prescribed specifically for you. However, in an emergency situation you may feel there is no alternative, in which case the information here can be used as a guide.

**APPENDICES · Field medicine**

# Dental care

Keeping your teeth clean will prevent painful mouth ailments and reduce the risk of an upset stomach. Put this at the end of your to-do list. Cavities are of more immediate concern.

- **Chew the end of a small stick into fibres.** The stick should be about the size of a pencil. The roots of a strawberry plant also work well.
- **Use the stick to massage gums and as a brush to remove food remnants.** Use once, then discard.
- **In place of toothpaste, use soap, salt or sand.** Or simply rinse with a saltwater mouthwash.
- **Fibre strands from the inside of tree bark can be used as dental floss.**

## Cavities

- **Make a temporary filling.** Painful cavities can be filled with a temporary filling material (such as Cavit). You simply wash and dry the tooth, roll the paste into a little ball and press into place. It takes about 15min to set, or roughly an hour at higher altitudes.
- **Use candle wax in the same manner as Cavit.** Wash and dry tooth well before filling with wax.
- **Use cotton wool and clove oil.** Put a drop of clove oil in a tablespoon of warm water, soak the cotton wool in this mix, twist into a tiny ball and wedge this onto the affected tooth.
- **Place a clove near the tooth and keep it in your mouth until pain abates.**

# Treating foot blisters

Blisters can become infected and lead to gangrene (and amputation). Ideally, you should stop and let the body repair itself before moving on.

## Prevention

- **Change socks frequently.**
- **Check your feet regularly for tender/sore spots.** Apply duct tape (a favourite trick of adventure racers) or white sports tape to those areas. Check the boot and sock for possible irritants.
- **Without tape or second-skin products, try lubricating the area with petroleum jelly or hand cream.** Adding an extra sock or even a piece from a plastic bag between the sore area and the shoe can help. Experiment with these techniques until the rubbing on the area is reduced.

## Treatment if continuing to walk

1. **Remove the entire blister.** Carefully cut away all the dead skin. This gives the raw skin below more exposure to the air, which will allow quicker healing.
2. **Clean with sterilizing fluid if available.**
3. **Give the blister as much time to dry out as possible before taping it up for travel.** If you've stopped travelling for the day, place a loose bandage on it overnight and wait until morning for proper taping.
4. **Bandage.** Use second skin (such as Compeed) on the blister and tape to decrease further irritation and change the dressing daily.
5. **Remove the tape during overnight breaks to let the wound dry and replace with dry, loose bandage.** Re-tape before moving on.

### Blister under toenail

When the toenail turns purple/black and becomes painful, it's time to puncture it.
1. **Heat puncture instrument.** Hold the end of a straightened paper clip or the dull end of a small sewing needle over a flame until glowing hot.
2. **Push it through the middle of the toenail.** This will puncture the blister and relieve the pressure. The heat of the metal will melt through the toenail, so you don't need a sharp point.

## Ingrown toenail

File down the middle of the toenail (from base to top). This thins the nail and weakens the middle, thus releasing pressure along the edges. It doesn't happen immediately. Wait a few hours before judging results.

## Heel crack

Feet easily dry out when wearing sandals and skin cracks are common, especially on the heel.
1. **Remove hard skin from surrounding area.** Use a footfile, sandpaper or a coarse rock. Soaking the foot first will make it easier to remove the skin.
2. **Clean the crack with soap, water and antiseptic.**
3. **Allow the foot to dry.**
4. **Superglue it shut.** Don't put the glue down at the bottom of the crack, just along the upper edge of the crack (a millimetre or two below the surface). Press together and add some more glue along the top of the crack. Hold shut until affixed. You can walk on it almost immediately.

5. **Use skin lotion to keep feet soft while the crack seals.** You may need to glue it back shut if it opens.

*This medical section was written in consultation with **Alistair Cole**, who served for eight years with the Parachute Regiment and Royal Army Medical Corps before becoming a mountain expedition leader, chief instructor of the Expedition Care Program, a fellow of the Royal Geographical Society and a qualified trauma medic. He has led over thirty overseas expeditions, and is now the Managing Director of The Lifesigns Group (@www.lifesignsgroup.co.uk), which conducts medical and safety training for independent travellers and expeditions.*

# 2: The survivor's mindset

"A survivor trusts himself and relies on himself. He or she is confident, but also humble. Survival is always a balancing act between opposing skills or forces. And when the crisis comes, he doesn't say, 'Oh, my God, how could this have happened to me?' A survivor doesn't complain or blame others. He or she says, 'OK, what's the next right thing to do to get out of this? I know that there is always one more thing I can do, and I'm going to do whatever it takes. I'm going to do my best.' That's survivor thinking." – Laurence Gonzales

1. **To win your battle against nature you first need to win a psychological battle against yourself.** It's smart to admit you're in an unfamiliar and dangerous situation (denial won't do you any good), but also understand that fear and panic want to take over in a crisis. Don't let them. They can drain your energy and allow you to give in to your feelings and imagination. Calm, cool thinking is the key. "If you run around saying, 'I'm going to die! I'm going to die! I'm going to die!'" says Robert Young Pelton (see p.148), "you probably will. The secret of survival is to stay calm and focus on what you know and what you can do."

2. **Take 5–10min to calm down and assess the situation.** The survival strategy at the beginning of each chapter will help walk you through these issues. Don't start moving for the sake of action. Don't make any hasty decisions. Stay put, stay relaxed and think. If you are stressed out and can't shake it, let your stress work for you. Stress can allow your hearing to become more sensitive and your sense of smell to become sharper. Even blood clotting becomes more effective under stress.

- Think about your physical condition, any equipment you may have and your food and water supply.
- Assess your surroundings. Look around for clues, landmarks, stars or sun direction.
- Can you hear any birds, an engine, voices?
- Can you detect any olfactory clues?
- Can you sense temperature changes or a cool breeze coming from a certain direction?

3. **Give yourself a pep talk.** Tell yourself that you're not going to let yourself die – you're going to make it. Your will to live is your ticket out. Find motivation. Fight for the sake of your family and friends. Here are a few ways to let the optimist in you shine through:
   - Use your sense of humour. "Who would have thought this was going to happen when I woke up this morning; I'm going to make a fortune writing a book about this when I get back!"
   - Look at the beauty of your surroundings. "If there was a guide here, I'd be paying to see this environment. Hey, I'm getting it for free!"
   - Celebrate your little successes along the way. "I made it across the stream! I got a fire started! I found a good landmark to keep me going in the right direction!"

4. **Think creatively to make use of the materials available to you.** A rock can be used as a hammer, a shiny CD to signal for help, dry grass and leaves stuffed in your clothing can keep you warm and a condom can be used to hold water.

5. **Keep an eye on your emotional level throughout.** Something as simple as not getting enough sleep can make trying to stay awake stressful (try to ensure you're getting at least 2hr sleep per 24). If you're staying in one spot for a while, sleep is a worthy goal. Spend the day preparing your bed and shelter and getting enough liquids so that you can get as much sleep as possible. Push aside sadness and frustration that can lead to depression and sap both your energy and will to survive. If you get angry, harness that energy and put it to use.

*This section was written in consultation with* **Laurence Gonzales**, *author of* Deep Survival. *Laurence is a contributing editor of* National Geographic Adventure Magazine, *for which he wrote the award-winning article "The 12 Rules of Survival".*

# 3: Rope, knots and traps

## Making rope

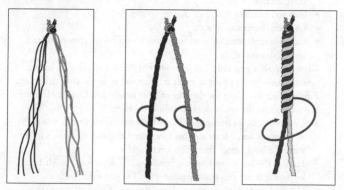

Find long, pliable grasses or strands of bark and rub them between the palms of your hands to remove debris. If only non-pliable vegetation (such as nettle stems) is available, soak it in water until supple, then pound with a stone to separate the good fibres from the pith. Leave the fibres to dry.

- Secure a batch of fibres with a knot at one end.
- Divide them into two even batches.
- Twist each batch in a clockwise direction.
- Twist the two twisted strands around each other in a counter clockwise direction.
- Splice in additional strands with twisting to add length as needed.
- Plait (braid) together 3 of these "ropes" to increase strength if needed. This is useful if you need extra strong cord to hold a person's weight or secure the main logs on a raft.

## Joining two ropes – sheet knot

Do not use a square/reef knot to join two ropes – it's not effective.

▲ Sheet knot

## Securing a rope to a fixed object – bowline

One of the most useful knots, this holds extremely well and is easy to untie after use, making it ideal for rescue when you need to hold someone's body weight.

▲ Bowline

## Butterfly knot

This is useful when you need to make a knot in the middle of a rope.

▲ Butterfly knot

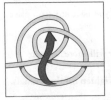  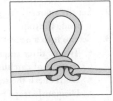

## Fastening sticks for an A-frame – sheer lashing

- **Tie a piece of rope around one of the poles.** Any simple knot will do, as it holds it in place while you begin lashing.
- **Wrap rope around both poles about 10 times.** Keep the tension, but do not make it too tight.

- **Wrap between the poles.** Do this a few times with tension.
- **End with a simple knot around one of the poles.** Make an extra knot or two just to be safe.

## Simple animal trap

1. **Make a snare loop.** Keep it small; you don't need or want to catch larger game, and smaller animals are more plentiful. Do this away from the area where you set the trap so you minimize your presence and smell there, which could frighten animals away. Wire works best as it's strong and can't be chewed through.

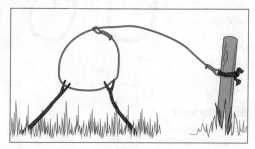

2. **Set the snare.** Try to put it on an animal trail. If you have any bait, place it beside the trap.
3. **Secure it to a nearby tree or stake.**
   - Two or three traps placed beside each other will increase your chances of catching something.
   - Don't check the traps too often or you will frighten off the animals.
   - Dismantle traps before you move on.

# 4: Navigation

## What to do when lost in the wilderness

- **Stay calm.** Sit down and collect your thoughts.
- **Look for clues.** Can you hear any noises? Cup both ears with your hands to help you hear in the direction you're looking, then slowly turn around. Smell anything? Remember, smells are often carried on the wind, so check wind direction.

- **Look for a nearby high point to get your bearings.** Take your gear with you so you don't lose that as well.
- **Find the trail.** If you've lost your trail, make increasingly larger circles from your position to relocate the trail (or your group's footprints).
- **Stay on used trails if available.** Don't leave them unless absolutely necessary.
- **Follow rivers downstream to reach civilization if unsure of direction.** This isn't a surefire approach, but a general guideline. Some streams disappear underground, others head into gorges and some larger, low-lying rivers make long swings with thick vegetation and muddy ground that makes for difficult traversing (and may be a good time to build a raft and float downstream).
- **Look for clues as you move.** Be aware of sounds, smells and major landmarks. Try to imagine what your route looks like from above and keep it in mind, or if you have paper and pen, draw it.
- **Mark your path in case you need to backtrack or a rescuer finds your trail.** Surveyor's tape (brightly coloured, easy to rip and cheap) is ideal. Using a stick or shoe to draw arrows in the ground is quick, helpful and has minimal environmental impact, but it's not much use in the rain or snow. Another method is to break branches and position stones in piles as you go. No matter what you do, look back frequently, as the terrain looks different on the return trip.

## Navigating with a watch

Knowing that the sun rises in the east and sets in the west won't help you determine direction when it's close to midday and the sun is high above. But knowing that at noon in the northern hemisphere the sun will be roughly due south, and roughly due north in the southern hemisphere, is useful. In the northern hemisphere at 6am the sun is due east, at 9am, it's southeast, at 3pm it's southwest and at 6pm it's due west. Vice versa for the southern hemisphere. To navigate on your time schedule, the quickest way to get a rough reading of north/south is with your watch (it's most accurate when it's close to noon). When the sun is high, and it's difficult to discern its precise direction, place a stick in the ground and look at the shadow. If you only have a digital watch, you still know the time, so imagine where the hour hand would be pointing on an analogue watch and estimate. Or, to help visualize, draw an analogue watch on paper.

### Northern hemisphere

1. **Point the hour hand of your watch at the sun.**
2. **South is halfway between the hour hand and 12.** If the watch is on daylight savings time (March–Sept) use the point halfway between the hour hand and 1.

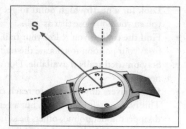

### Southern hemisphere

1. **Point the 12 on your watch at the sun.**
2. **North is halfway between the 12 and the hour hand.** If the watch is on daylight savings time (Oct–March) imagine the hour hand is one hour behind and use that to make your calculation.

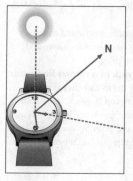

## Navigating by the sun's shadow

This is slightly more accurate than the watch method above, but not absolute, and takes about 20min to get a reading. You'll get more accurate results using this method when it's closer to noon.

1. **Place a knee- or waist-high stick in the ground on a flat surface.** Let it cast an unobstructed shadow.
2. **Mark the end of the shadow.** This is the western mark in the northern hemisphere or eastern mark in the southern hemisphere.
3. **Wait 20min.** Don't touch the stick during this period. Around noon, when the sun is straight overhead, you may need to wait longer than 20min for a reading.

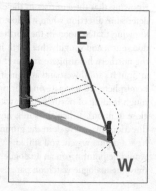

4. **Mark the end of the new shadow.** This is the eastern mark in the northern hemisphere or western mark in the southern hemisphere.
5. **Draw a line between the first and second markings.** That will provide you with an east-west line.

## Navigating by the stars

### Locating north in the northern hemisphere

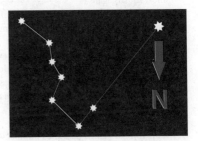

1. **Locate the Plough (Big Dipper).** Draw an imaginary line between the two stars at the end of the Plough's bowl. The distance to the North Star is about five times the distance between the two stars in the Plough you are using to spot it.

2. **Draw an imaginary line straight down to the ground to create a northern landmark.** From anywhere in the northern hemisphere, the North Star is due north.

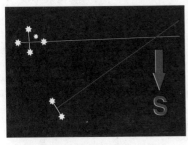

### Locating south in the southern hemisphere

1. **Find the Southern Cross.** It's a group of five stars in the shape of a cross and tilted to one side (it's not as easy to spot as the Plough). There are two bright "pointer stars" that can help direct you towards it.

2. **Imagine the long axis extends in a line five times the length of the cross.** The end of that imaginary line is south.

3. **Draw an imaginary line straight down to the ground to create a southern landmark.**

# 5: Signalling

## Giving the international distress signal

- **Signal SOS.** SOS is three short signals, three long signals, then three short signals again (– – – — — — – – –). This can be signalled in any way, including beeps and flashes. The simple version of the emergency signal is three (six in Europe), for example, three (six) whistle blasts, light blinks, smoke puffs, etc.

- **Radio**. Transmitting radios typically have a range of 32km. Wait for a plane or boat sighting before using; otherwise use sparingly to save batteries. The frequencies (typically preset) should be at 121.5MHz or 406MHz, VHF channel 70 or 16. The military frequency is 253MHz.
  **What to say:**
  Mayday, mayday, mayday.
  This is [boat's name or plane's number – repeat 3 times].
  Mayday.
  This is [boat's name or plane's number].
  My position is [give exact location or landmark or say you don't know].
  I am [lost/injured/adrift at sea, etc].
  I have [number of people in your party, x amount of water left, flares].
  I require immediate assistance.
  Over.

- **Wave a light.** If aiming your torch (flashlight) at a plane or boat, wave the light back and forth slowly in a steady motion. The most important thing is that you're not pointing a beam at the rescuer's face.

## Signalling with a mirror

A glass signalling mirror with US military specs is ideal, but any mirror or reflective surface can be used for signalling. Try a CD or even the hologram on a credit card if that's all you've got.

### With a signalling mirror

Follow any directions that come with the mirror. Look through the hole in the back of the mirror. Aim the centre at the aeroplane or boat you're trying to signal. Practise on a fixed object at close range so you can see you're hitting your target.

### With a basic reflective object

Extend one arm and put the object you wish to signal within a V formed with your fingers. Keep a glimmer of shine on your hand so you know you're probably hitting your target. Practise on a fixed object at close range.

## Mobile phones

If you're not getting reception, move to higher ground or into a clearing, away from trees and other large objects. See p.202 for emergency numbers.

## Firing a flare gun

- **Fire a flare only when the rescue plane/boat is headed in your direction.** Once it has passed by, the flare is wasted.
- **Fire straight up when there's no wind.**
- **Aim the gun 15 degrees from straight up in the downwind direction when windy.**
- **Fire at a 45-degree angle downwind with low clouds.**

## Making ground markings

- **Write an "X" (international emergency signal) or "SOS".**
- **Make the letter/s no less than 6m tall and 2m wide.**
- **Maximize contrast of colours.** Use dark logs on a white beach, for example.

## Signal fires

- **Make a bright fire.** Keep one fire going and have an extra fire or two ready to start immediately (see p.198 for fire starting) or at least extra tinder to add to your primary fire to increase the flame.
- **Make white smoke.** Burn green vegetation (leaves and grasses) to create white smoke when there's a dark background.

- **Make dark smoke.** Burn oil products (rubber, plastic, tyres) to create dark smoke when there's a light background. Be careful not to inhale toxic fumes.

## Getting seen while on the move

- **Walk out in the open when possible.** But make sure you're not at risk from the sun, wind or storms.
- **Wear colours that contrast with your surroundings.**
- **Affix shiny objects to your pack at different angles:** jewellery, CDs, aluminium foil, etc.
- **Leave clues that can be seen from the air.** In snow and sand write out giant letters with your feet.
- **Make a big "SOS" with an arrow showing the direction you are heading in.**
- **Burn a lone tree.** Make sure the tree is set very far apart from any others and there's no flammable debris around and the wind will not carry sparks into a wooded area. Extreme caution must be taken not to start a forest fire. Before leaving the burning tree, mark the direction you are travelling on the ground with stones or sticks.

## Getting rescued by helicopter

- **Find a clearing at least 35m wide.** The larger, the better.
- **Mark the centre with a big "X".**
- **Remove debris that could get whipped up by the rotor.** If in the snow, tramp down as large an area as possible.
- **Show the wind direction.** Hang a bright scarf on a nearby stick so the pilot can gauge the wind.
- **Stand 30m from the centre "X".** Keep your back to the wind and your arm pointed to the "X".

## How to tell you've been spotted

Those you are signalling may let you know that they've seen you in one of the following ways:

- **Dropping orange smoke.**
- **Rocking the plane's wings up and down.**
- **Firing three white flares or making three loud noises at one-minute intervals.**

# 6: Testing plants for poison

Because most people are rescued within three days, food is unlikely to be an issue (you can survive for about three weeks without it). However, if you happen to find food you can positively identify, don't miss the chance to eat if you have plenty of water to digest it. More than half of all plants are poisonous to humans or just inedible. Of those that are edible, it's usually only a single part of the plant that can be eaten. Because testing takes some time and effort, it's most worthwhile if you choose a plant that is in abundance so that you'll have a good supply if it's safe to eat. That doesn't mean it should become your only nutrients; even if it's safe in moderate quantities, too much of some plants is not good for you.

Here are some points to consider when choosing a plant to go for:
- Do not assume that plants are safe because animals are eating them.
- Brightly coloured plants are more likely to be poisonous.
- Very pungent smells often indicate poison.

## Poison test

1. **Skin contact test.** Crush a leaf or berry of the plant and rub it on the skin of your inner wrist. If no itching, blistering or burning occurs after 15min, proceed to step 2.
2. **Mouth contact test.** Place a small amount of the crushed item between your gum and lower lip. Leave it there for 5min. If there are no unpleasant reactions, proceed to step 3.
3. **Chew test.** Chew the item. If there's no burning, soapy taste or extreme bitterness, proceed to step 4.
4. **Swallow test.** Swallow some of the juice after chewing the item, but not the pulp. Wait 8hr. If there are no cramps, sleeplessness or dizziness, proceed to step 5.
5. **Eat test (small sample).** Eat a teaspoon-size amount of the leaves or berries of the plant. Wait another 8hr for similar symptoms to those in step 4. If none, proceed to step 6.
6. **Eat test (larger sample).** Eat a handful of the leaves or berries of the plant and wait 24hr. If there are still no symptoms, you may assume the item is safe to consume.

### Mushrooms

The poison test does not work for mushrooms. All mushrooms should be avoided unless you're confident that you can correctly identify them as edible.

# 7: Starting fires

See p.82 for starting fires without firewood or kindling and, p.195 for creating smoke.

## Teepee fire

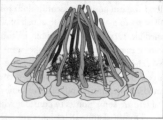

**Time:** 5–20min.
**Gear:**
- About three handfuls of tinder:
  crushed dry leaves, dry moss,
  dry bark, dry grass, tiny slivers
  of dry sticks, cotton balls
  covered in petroleum jelly, lint,
  bird down, dried inner bits of dead trees, sawdust, wood shavings,
  oil/gas-soaked cloths, tampons, photographic film, birds' nest material.
- A handful of kindling.
- Sticks the thickness of pens, heavy cardboard.
- Larger sticks and some logs. Keep damp wood near the fire to let it dry
  out. Bamboo explodes when heated while others, such as willow, only
  smoulder.
- Matches or other lighting equipment.
- 6–12 freshly cut green sticks (when there's snow on the ground).

**Directions:**
1. **Prepare the ground.** Clear away any debris from a small, flat area about
   the size of a chess board to form your fire pit. Where forest fires are
   prevalent (there's plenty of dry, flammable debris) clear an area that's 4m
   from the fire in every direction. Don't build it too close to trees and do
   not surround the fire with wet rocks as these can actually explode as they
   heat up. The fire doesn't need to be built on dry rocks, but this will be
   useful if making a hot bed (see p.43).
2. **Keep the fire from sinking if on snow.** Lay a row of green sticks on the
   ground and build your fire on top of that.
3. **Make a small pile of tinder.** Make sure it's not too compact and that
   the most flammable bits are on the bottom. If you have any special tinder
   cubes from a survival kit or have made your own (cotton balls or tampons
   covered with petroleum jelly, then slightly pulled apart), place them with
   the tinder.

4. **Lean small sticks together over the tinder to form a teepee.** Don't smother the tinder, build just over it. Alternatively, put the sticks in place first, then add the tinder inside as if building a nest.
5. **Place continually larger sticks on the outside of the teepee.**
6. **Ignite.**
7. **Carefully add more tinder and kindling until the flame catches on the teepee.**
8. **The teepee will eventually collapse when the fire gets going.** At this point the fire is ideal for cooking over.

## In windy conditions

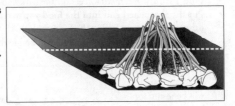

- **Look for shelter just behind a natural wind block.**
- **Dig a pit in a swimming-pool shape, deeper at one end.** Build the teepee over the "deep end" and feed fuel in from the "shallow end". Stack up rocks or a large log on the windy side to create an additional block.

## In arctic areas and at night

- **Start by making a contained flame.** Use a candle or flammable material in a metal can so you can see what you're doing in the dark and keep the melting snow from dousing your flame.
- **Place the tinder over the candle or flammable material until it ignites.** Keep the kindling and larger wood to hand so you don't waste precious heat from the burning tinder.

## Fire lighting

- **Stab damp wooden matches onto the striker at an angle instead of drawing them along the surface.**
- **Use a magnifying glass to focus the sun on your tinder.** Very fine, dry tinder is vital.
- **Use a large battery and jump leads (jumper cables).** After connecting the leads to the battery and starting the vehicle, touch the other end of

the leads together just beside the tinder to create a spark. Be careful not to spark the cables near the car battery where gases can cause an explosion.

## Cooking over a fire

Without proper camping equipment, cooking over an open fire is difficult if you use the flame itself. Food can burn quickly and it's easy to get burnt yourself while moving metal cans placed close to the fire. But the flame does provide warmth and light for cooking.

- **Use a stick to rake some hot embers aside to form a small cooking area.**
- **Find a sturdy green stick.** Peel off the bark and sharpen at one end.
- **Put the sharpened end into the food you're cooking and hold the other end.** If you're letting the food cook slowly, sharpen the stick at both ends and push one end into the ground beside the fire so that the food dangles over the fire. A rock and a Y-shaped stick will be useful for heavier food.

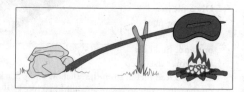

## Carrying fire

If you're on the move and don't have matches or a lighter to start a fire easily, you may wish to carry burning embers with you to ensure you can make a fire quickly at your next stop.

1. **Find a tin can and tie a string (wire is even better) to the upper rim so you can carry it.**
2. **Make a few holes in the bottom third of the can to help get oxygen to the coals.**
3. **Gather dry moss and (if possible) some twigs from a birch tree and line the can with them.**
4. **Place a few half-burnt bits of charcoal from the edge of your recent fire into the moss nest.**
5. **Cover with more moss and birch.**
6. **Pack carefully.** If the embers are packed too tightly they may be extinguished due to lack of oxygen. If packed too loosely, the moss may catch fire.
7. **Check regularly on the coals.** Blow on them a bit to keep them smouldering.

**Leaving a fire**

Always maintain a safe fire pit and extinguish the fire before moving on.
- **Dose with water if you have an abundance.**
- **Do not cover with dirt.** This can slow the burning by limiting oxygen supply, but keep the embers alive.
- **Simply quit adding fuel to the fire well before you leave.**
- **Mix remnants of the fire with cool, moist dirt (dug up from below the surface) or mud and stir until there is no heat coming form the pile of earth.**

# 8: Water disinfection

Clear water should be disinfected. Murky water with particles should be filtered first, then disinfected. This is not just for drinking water, also for brushing teeth and cooking. If you find water but can't filter or disinfect it, it's better to drink it and risk catching a waterborne disease than dehydrate. Distilling (using the sun's rays to heat the water and then trap the vapours or let them condense into drops) filters and disinfects at once, but even a good still will produce only about 2–3dl (1 cup) of water in a day, which will not meet your water requirements in just about any environment. The various chapters cover other condition-specific techniques for finding drinkable water.

## Filtering drinking water

- **Find a makeshift filter (coffee filter, shirt, bandana) or make a simple filter.** Place clean grass, sand, pebbles or moss, or any combination of these, in a container that has several holes in the bottom.
- **Pour the water through the filter several times.** This applies to any "homemade" filter you use.

## Purifying by boiling

- **As a guideline, boil water for 1min at sea level and a couple of minutes at higher altitudes.**
- **Use a cover to prevent evaporation.**

## Purifying with any of the following chemicals

Do not use a combination of these chemicals.

* **Use water tablets or drops if you have them and follow directions.**
* **Use 5 drops of regular (2 percent tincture) iodine per litre of clear water (10 drops for cloudy water).** Let stand for 30min. This isn't advisable for pregnant women, people with thyroid conditions or those allergic to iodine.
* **Use chlorine bleach.** For each litre of water, add 10 drops of 1 percent chlorine or 2 drops of 4–6 percent chlorine or 1 drop of 7–10 percent chlorine. If unknown, use 10 drops. Use unscented bleach only. Wait 30min after adding the bleach. If the water doesn't have a slight "bleach" odour to it, repeat process before drinking. To make the taste more palatable, let it stand for several hours or pour back and forth between two containers several times.

*This section was written in consultation with* **Cody Lundin**, *the chief instructor and founder of the Aboriginal Living Skills School (⊛ www.alssadventures.com) in Prescott, Arizona. Cody also serves as an adjunct faculty member at Yavapai College and the Ecosa Institute. He is the author of* 98.6 Degrees: The Art of Keeping Your Ass Alive!

# 9: Emergency numbers

Each telephone number below appears as you would dial it within that country. The number in brackets is the city code where the embassy is located. If you are in the same city as the embassy, you may not need this number. When you get referred to another country, begin dialling the international call with the numbers in that box and continue with the local number found for your embassy in the corresponding box. When making an international call, you may need to omit any number before the city code in brackets. For example, when calling the Australian Embassy in Islamabad, Pakistan (listed in the box below as 0 (51) 2824345 ), you dial 2824345 in Islamabad, 0 512824345 from anywhere in the country except Islamabad, and from outside the country, you dial the number you need to make an international call, then the country code (92 in this case), then the number. From Sydney, Australia, to this embassy, it would be 0011 92 512824345 (notice the "0" preceding the "51" has been dropped for this international call).

| Country | Emergency phone number | US Embassies | UK Embassies | Australian Embassies | Canadian Embassies | New Zealand Embassies |
|---|---|---|---|---|---|---|
| Afghanistan | | 0 (20) 290002 | 0 (70) 102000 | Call embassy in Pakistan (0092+) | 0 (70) 294281 | Call embassy in Pakistan (0092+) |
| Albania | 19 | 0 (4) 247285 | 0 (4) 234973 | | 0 (4) 257274 | |
| Algeria | | 7 (21) 691255 extn 7019 | 7 (21) 230068 | | 7 (21) 914951 or 914960 | Call embassy in France (0033+) |
| Andorra | 110 | Call embassy in Spain (0034+) | Call embassy in Spain (0034+) | Call embassy in Spain (0034+) | Call embassy in Spain (0034+) | Call embassy in Spain (0034+) |
| Argentina | 101 | 0 (11) 57774533 | 0 (11) 48082200 | 0 (11) 47793500 | 0 (11) 48081000 | 0 (11) 43280747 |
| Armenia | | 8 (10) 520791 | 8 (10) 264301 | | 8 (10) 567990 | |
| Australia | 000 (112 from mobile phone) | 0 (2) 62145600 | 0 (2) 62706666 | | 0 (2) 62704000 | 0 (2) 62704211 |
| Angola | | 0 (2) 345481 | 0 (2) 334582 | 0 (2) 335561 | 0 (2) 448371/66/77 | |
| Austria | 112 | 0 (1) 313390 | 0 (1) 716130 | 0 (1) 506740 | 0 (1) 531383910 | 0 (1) 3188505 |
| Bosnia | 92 | 0 (33) 445700 | | 0 (33) 251230 | 0 (33) 222033 | Call embassy in Italy (0039+) |
| Bahrain | 999 | 0 17242700 | 0 179600274 | | Call embassy in Saudi Arabia (00966+) | Call embassy in Saudi Arabia (00966+) |
| Bangladesh | 866 551-3 | 0 (2) 8813440 | 0 (2) 8822705 | 0 (2) 881 3101 | 0 (2) 9887091/97 | Call embassy in India (0091+) |
| Barbados | 112/119 | 1 4366300 | 1 4307800 | | 1 4293550 | Call embassy in Canada (001+) |

| Country | Emergency phone number | US Embassies | UK Embassies | Australian Embassies | Canadian Embassies | New Zealand Embassies |
|---|---|---|---|---|---|---|
| Belarus | 02 | 8 (172) 315000 | 8 (172) 105920/1 | | Call embassy in Poland (0048+) | Call embassy in Russia (007+) |
| Belgium | 112 | 0 (2) 5082111 | 0 (2) 2876211 | 0 (2) 2860500 | 0 (2) 7410611 | 0 (2) 5121040 |
| Belize | 911 | 0 (2) 77161 | 0 (82) 22146 | | 0 (2) 31060 | |
| Bolivia | 911 | 0 (2) 2168000 | 0 (2) 2433424 | 0 (2) 2440459 | 0 (2) 2415021 | |
| Botswana | 997/911 | 353982 | 3952841 | | 3904411 | Call embassy in South Africa (0027+) |
| Brazil | 911 | 0 (61) 3217272 | 0 (61) 3292300 | 0 (61) 226311 | 0 (61) 4245400 | 0 (61) 2489900 |
| Burkina Faso | | | 50307323 | Call Canadian embassy | 50311894 50311895/50312585 | |
| Cambodia | 119 | 0 (23) 216436 | 0 (23) 427124 | 0 (23) 213470 | 0 (23) 213470 | Call embassy in Thailand (0066+) |
| Cameroon | | | 2220545/2220796 | Call Canadian embassy | 2232311 | |
| Canada | 911 | 1 (613) 2385335 | | 1 (613) 2360841 | | 1 (613) 2385991 |
| China | 110 | 0 (10) 65323831 | 0 (10) 51924000 | 0 (10) 65322331 | 0 (10) 65323536 | 0 (10) 65322731 |
| Colombia | 119 | 0 (1) 3150811 | 0 (1) 3268300 | 0 (1) 2180942 | 0 (1) 6579800 | 0 (93) 2307795 |
| Costa Rica | 911 | 2203939 | 2582025 | Call Canadian embassy | 2424400 | |
| Croatia | 112 | 0 (1) 4555500 | 0 (1) 6009122 | 0 (1) 4891200 | 0 (1) 4881211 | 0 (1) 6151382 |

| Country | Emergency phone number | US Embassies | UK Embassies | Australian Embassies | Canadian Embassies | New Zealand Embassies |
|---|---|---|---|---|---|---|
| Cuba | 26811 | 0 (7) 8333552 | 0 (7) 2041771 | Call Canadian embassy | 0 (7) 2042516/17 | Call embassy in Mexico (0052+) |
| Cyprus | 112 | 22393939 | 22861100 | 22753001 | 2775508/777000 | 22818884 |
| Czech Republic | 158 | (2) 57530663 | (2) 57402111 | (2) 96578350 | (2) 72101800 | (2) 22514672 |
| Denmark | 112 | 35553144 | 35445200 | 70263676 | 33483200 | 33377702 |
| Democratic republic of Congo | | 0 (81) 2255871 | 0 (98) 337007 | Call Canadian embassy | 0 (88)50310 or 50311 | |
| Dominican Republic | 911 | 1 2215511 | 1 4727111 | | 1 6851136 | |
| East Timor | 112 | | 3322838 | 3322111 | | 7230928 |
| Ecuador | 101 | 0 (2) 2562890 | 0 (2) 2970800 | 0 (4) 2680700 | 0 (2) 2232114 | |
| Egypt | | 0 (2) 3557371 | 0 (92) 794050 or 7940852 | 0 (2) 5750444 | 0 (2) 7943110 | 0 (2) 5749360 |
| El Salvador | 911 | 2786020 | Call embassy in Guatemala (00502+) | | 2794655/2794657 | Call embassy in Mexico (0052+) |
| Equatorial Guinea | | Call embassy in Cameroon (00237+) | Call embassy in Cameroon (00237+) | | Call embassy in Gabon (00241+) | |
| Eritrea | | 0 (1) 120004 | 0 (1) 120145 | | 0 (1) 181940 | |
| Estonia | 110 | 6688100 | 6674700 | 6509308 | 627311/6273310 | Call embassy in the Netherlands (0031+) |
| Ethiopia | | 0 (1) 550066 | 0 (1) 612354 | Call Canadian embassy | 0 (1) 713022 | |

| Country | Emergency phone number | US Embassies | UK Embassies | Australian Embassies | Canadian Embassies | New Zealand Embassies |
|---|---|---|---|---|---|---|
| Fiji | 000/911 | 0 3314466 | 0 3229100 | 0 3382211 | 0 6722400 | 0 3311422 |
| Finland | 112 | 0 (9) 171931 | 0 (2) 2865284 | 0 (9) 47776640 | 0 (9) 228530 | 0 (2) 4701818 |
| France | 112 | 0 (1) 43122222 | 0 (1) 44513100 | 0 (1) 40593300 | 0 (1) 44432900 | 0 (1) 45014343 |
| Gabon | | 762003 | See embassy in Cameroon (00237+) | Call Canadian embassy | 737354 | |
| Gambia | 17 | 4392856 | 4495133 or 4495134 | | See embassy in Senegal (00221+) | |
| Georgia | 02 | | 8 (32) 955497 or 998447 | | See embassy in Turkey (0090+) | |
| Germany | 112 | 0 (30) 83050 | 0 (30) 204570 | 0 (30) 8800880 | 0 (30) 203120 | 0 (30) 206 210 |
| Ghana | | 0 (21) 229179 | 0 (21)/0110650 or 221665 | 0 (21) 781979 or 781980 | 0 (21) 211521 | |
| Greece | 112/100 | (21) 7202303 | (21) 07272600 | (21) 8704000 | (21) 7273400 | (21) 06874700 |
| Grenada | | 1 4441173 | 1 4403536 or 4403222 | | Call embassy in Barbados (001246+) | |
| Guatemala | 110 | 3311541 | 23675425 | Call Canadian embassy | 23634348 | 4313742 |
| Guinea | | 0 4754400 | 0 455807 | Call Canadian embassy | 0 462395 | |
| Guinea-Bissau | | | Call embassy in Senegal (00221+) | | | |
| Guyana | 999 | 0 (225) 4900 | 0 (226) 5881 | | 0 (227) 2081 or 2082 | |

| Country | Emergency phone number | US Embassies | UK Embassies | Australian Embassies | Canadian Embassies | New Zealand Embassies |
|---|---|---|---|---|---|---|
| Haiti | 114 | 0 2220200 | 0 2573969 | | 0 2983066 | |
| Honduras | 119 | 0 2369320 or 0 2385114 | Call embassy in Guatemala (00502+) | | 0 2324551 | |
| Hungary | 112 | 06 (1) 4754400 | 06 (1) 2662888 | 06 (1) 457 9777 | 06 (1) 3923360 | 06 (1) 302 2484 /2613 |
| Iceland | 112 | 0 5629100 | 0 5505100 | | 0 5756500 | |
| India | | 0 (11) 6889033 | 0 (11) 26872161 | 0 (11) 51399900 | 0 (11) 51782000 | 0 (11) 26883170 |
| Indonesia | 110 | 0 (21) 3442211 | 0 (21) 3156264 | 0 (21) 25505555 | 0 (21) 25507800 | 0 (21) 5709460 |
| Iran | 129 | | 0 (21) 6705011 | 0 (21) 8724456 | 0 (21) 8732623 or 8732624 | 0 (21) 2800289 or 2800290 or 2800291 |
| Iraq | | 0 (240) 5530584 | 0 (1) 7901926280 | 0 (1) 7782210 or 7782225 or 7782215 | Call embassy in Jordan (00962+) | |
| Ireland | 999 | 0 (1) 6668777 | 0 (1) 2053700 | 0 (1) 6645300 | 0 (1) 4174100 | Call embassy in UK (0044+) |
| Israel | 100 | 0 (3) 519575 | 0 (3) 7251222 | 0 (3) 6950451 | 0 (3) 6363300 | |
| Italy | 112 | (03) 32245000 | (06) 42200001 | (06) 852721 | (06) 68307316 | |
| Ivory Coast | | 0 22494000 | 0 20300800 | Call Canadian embassy | 20300700 | |
| Jamaica | 119 | 1 9294850 | 1 5100700 | | 1 92615007 | Call embassy in Canada (001+) |
| Japan | 110 | 0 (3) 32245000 | 0 (3) 52111100 | 0 (3) 5232 4111 | 0 (3) 54126200 | 0 (3) 3467 2271 |

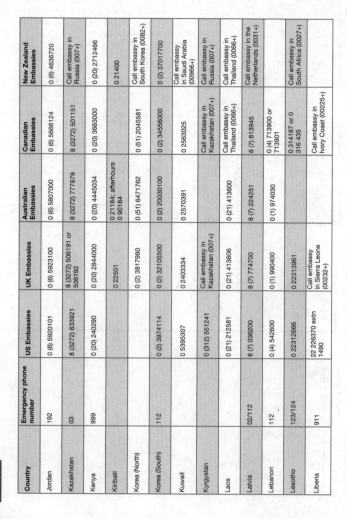

| Country | Emergency phone number | US Embassies | UK Embassies | Australian Embassies | Canadian Embassies | New Zealand Embassies |
|---|---|---|---|---|---|---|
| Jordan | 192 | 0 (6) 5920101 | 0 (6) 5923100 | 0 (6) 5807000 | 0 (6) 5666124 | 0 (6) 4636720 |
| Kazakhstan | 03 | 8 (3272) 633921 | 8 (3272) 506191 or 506192 | 8 (3272) 777879 | 8 (3272) 501151 | Call embassy in Russia (007+) |
| Kenya | 999 | 0 (20) 240290 | 0 (20) 2844000 | 0 (20) 4445034 | 0 (20) 3663000 | 0 (20) 2712466 |
| Kiribati | | | 0 22501 | 0 21184; afterhours 0 90184 | | 0 21400 |
| Korea (North) | | | 0 (2) 3817980 | 0 (51) 6471762 | 0 (51) 2045581 | Call embassy in South Korea (0082+) |
| Korea (South) | 112 | 0 (2) 3974114 | 0 (2) 32105500 | 0 (2) 20030100 | 0 (2) 34556000 | 0 (2) 37017700 |
| Kuwait | | 0 5395307 | 0 2403334 | 0 2570391 | 0 2563025 | Call embassy in Saudi Arabia (00966+) |
| Kyrgystan | | 0 (312) 551241 | Call embassy in Kazakhstan (007+) | | Call embassy in Kazakhstan (007+) | Call embassy in Russia (007+) |
| Laos | | 0 (21) 212581 | 0 (21) 413606 | 0 (21) 413600 | Call embassy in Thailand (0066+) | Call embassy in Thailand (0066+) |
| Latvia | 02/112 | 8 (7) 036200 | 8 (7) 774700 | 8 (7) 224251 | 8 (7) 813945 | Call embassy in the Netherlands (0031+) |
| Lebanon | 112 | 0 (4) 542600 | 0 (1) 990400 | 0 (1) 974030 | 0 (4) 713900 or 713901 | |
| Lesotho | 123/124 | 0 22312666 | 0 22313961 | | 0 314187 or 0 316 435 | Call embassy in South Africa (0027+) |
| Liberia | 911 | 22 226370 extn 1490 | Call embassy in Sierra Leone (00232+) | | Call embassy in Ivory Coast (00225+) | |

| Country | Emergency phone number | US Embassies | UK Embassies | Australian Embassies | Canadian Embassies | New Zealand Embassies |
|---|---|---|---|---|---|---|
| Libya | | | 0 (21) 3403644/5 | | 0 (21) 3351633 | |
| Liechtenstein | 112 | | Call embassy in Switzerland (0041+) | | Call embassy in Switzerland (0041+) | Call embassy in the Netherlands (0031+) |
| Lithuania | 112 | 8 (2) 223031 | 8 (5) 2462900 | 8 (5) 2123369 | 8 (5) 2490950 | |
| Luxembourg | 112/113 | 460123 | 229864 | Call embassy in Belgium (0032+) | 26270570 | Call embassy in Belgium (0032+) |
| Macedonia | 92 | 0 (2) 3116180; after hours 0 (70) 205687 | 0 (2) 3299299 | 0 (2) 361114 | Call embassy in Serbia and Montenegro (00381+) | |
| Madagascar | | 0 (22) 21257 or 0 (22) 21258 | 0 (22) 49378 or 0 (22) 49379 | | 0 (22) 42559 | |
| Malawi | 997 | 1773166 | 1772400 | | 645441 or 645269 | |
| Malaysia | 999 | 0 (3) 21685000 | 0 (3) 21702200 | 0 (3) 21465555 | 0 (3) 27183333 | 0 (3) 20782533 |
| Maldives | 119 | | Call embassy in Sri Lanka (0094+) | | | |
| Mali | 18 | 0 2225470 | Call embassy in Senegal (00221+) | Call Canadian embassy | 0 2212236 | |
| Malta | 112 | 0 25614000 | 0 23230000 | 0 21338201 | 0 25523233 | 0 21435025 |
| Marshall Islands | | 1 (247) 4011 | Call embassy in Fiji (00679+) | | | |
| Mauritania | 117 | 0 5252660 or 0 5252663 | Call embassy in Morocco (00212+) | | Call embassy in Morocco (00212+) | |

| Country | Emergency phone number | US Embassies | UK Embassies | Australian Embassies | Canadian Embassies | New Zealand Embassies |
|---|---|---|---|---|---|---|
| Mauritius | 066 | 0 2082347 | 0 2029400 | 0 2020160 | Call embassy in South Africa (0027+) | 0 2664920 or 0 2865579 |
| Mexico | | 01 (55) 52099100 | 01 (55) 52428500 | 01 (55) 11012200 | 01 (55) 57247900 | 01 (55) 52839460 |
| Micronesia | | | Call embassy in Fiji (00679+) | | | |
| Moldova | 902 | 0 (2) 233772 | 0 (2) 238991 | | Call embassy in Romania (0040+) | |
| Monaco | 112 | | 0 93509954 | | 0 97706242 | |
| Mongolia | 102 | 0 (11) 329095 | 0 (11) 458133 | | 0 (11) 328 285 | Call embassy in China (0086+) |
| Morocco | 19 | (37) 762265 | (37) 729696 | Call Canadian embassy | (37) 687400 | Call embassy in Spain (0034+) |
| Mozambique | 197 | 0 (1) 492797 | 0 (1) 320111 | 0 (1) 322780 | 0 (1) 492623 | Call embassy in South Africa (0027+) |
| Namibia | 1011 | 0 (61) 221601 | 0 (61) 274800 | | 0 (61) 227417 | 0 (61) 225228 |
| Nepal | 100 | 0 (1) 411179 | 0 (1) 4410583 | 0 (1) 4371678 | 0 (1) 415193 | 0 (1) 4412436 |
| Netherlands | 112 | 0 (70) 3109209 | 0 (70) 4270427 | 0 (70) 3108200 | 0 (70) 3111600 | 0 (70) 3469324 |
| New Zealand | 111 | 0 (4) 4626000 | 0 (4) 9242888 | 0 (4) 4736411 | 0 (4) 4739577 | |
| Nicaragua | 118 | 0 (2) 680123 | Call embassy in Costa Rica (00506+) | | | |
| Niger | | 0 722661 | Call embassy in Ivory Coast (00225+) | Call Canadian embassy | 0 753686 or 753687 | |

210

| Country | Emergency phone number | US Embassies | UK Embassies | Australian Embassies | Canadian Embassies | New Zealand Embassies |
|---|---|---|---|---|---|---|
| Nigeria | | 0 (9) 5230916 | 0 (1) 2619531 | 0 (9) 4135226 | 0 (9) 4139910 | Call embassy in UK (0044+) |
| Norway | 112/110 | 22448550 | 23132700 | 67584848 | 22995300 | 67110033 |
| Oman | 999 | 0 698989 | 0 609000 | | Call embassy in Saudi Arabia (00966+) | 0 794932 or 795726 |
| Pakistan | | 0 (51) 2080000 | 0 (51) 2822131 | 0 (51) 2824345 | 0 (51) 2086000 | 0 (21) 5656993 or 0 (21) 5656994 |
| Panama | 104 | 0 2077000 | 0 2690866 | | 0 2649731 | |
| Papua New Guinea | 000 | | 3251643 | 3259333 (24hr) | 262733844 | 3259444 |
| Paraguay | 00 | 0 (21) 213715 | 0 (21) 612611 | | 0 (21) 227207 | Call embassy in Argentina (0054+) |
| Peru | 011/5114 | 0 (1) 4343000 | 0 (1) 6173000 | 0 (1) 2228281 | 0 (1) 4444015 | 0 (1) 4227491 |
| Philippines | 166/117 | 0 (2) 5286300 | 0 (2) 8167116 | 0 (2) 7578100 | 0 (2) 8579000 | 0 (2) 8915358 |
| Poland | 112/999 | 0 (22) 6283041 | 0 (22) 3110000 | 0 (22) 5213444 | 0 (22) 5843100 | 0 (22) 5210500 |
| Portugal | 112 | 217273300 | 213924000 | 213101500 | 213164600 | Call embassy in Italy (0039+) |
| Qatar | 999/118 | 0 4884101 | 0 4421991 | | Call embassy in Kuwait (00965+) | Call embassy in Saudi Arabia (00966+) |
| Romania | 955 | 0 (21) 3164052 | 0 (21) 2017200 | 0 (1) 3209802 | 0 (21) 3075077 | |
| Russia | 112 | 8 (095) 7285577 | 8 (095) 9567200 | 8 (095) 9566070 | 8 (095) 1056000 | 8 (095) 9563579 or 9563580 |

| Country | Emergency phone number | US Embassies | UK Embassies | Australian Embassies | Canadian Embassies | New Zealand Embassies |
|---|---|---|---|---|---|---|
| Rwanda | | 0 505601 or 505602 | 0 585771 or 585773 | | 0 573210 or 573278 | |
| St Kitts and Nevis | 911 | | 4620008 | | Call embassy in Barbados (001246+) | |
| St Lucia | 999 / 911 | | 4522484 | | Call embassy in Barbados (001246+) | |
| St Vincent | 999/911 | | 1 (784) 4571701 | | Call embassy in Barbados (001246+) | |
| Samoa | 911 | | 9242888 | 23411 | | 21711 |
| San Marino | 112 | | Call embassy in Italy (0039+) | | Call embassy in Italy (0039+) | |
| Sao Tome and Principe | | | Call embassy in Angola (00244+) | | Call embassy in Gabon (00241+) | |
| Saudi Arabia | 999 | 0 (1) 4883800 | 0 (1) 4880077 | 0 (1) 4887788 | 0 (1) 4882288 or 4882289 | 0 (1) 4887988 |
| Senegal | | 0 8696300 | 0 8237392 or 8239971 | Call Canadian embassy | 0 8894700 | |
| Serbia and Montenegro | | 0 (11) 645655 | 0 (11) 264055 | 0 (11) 624655 | 0 (11) 3063000 | |
| Seychelles | | | 0 283666 | | Call embassy in Tanzania (00255+) | |
| Sierra Leone | | 0 (22) 226481 extn 249 | 0 (22) 232961 | | Call embassy in Guinea (00224+) | |
| Singapore | 999 | 64769100 | 64244200 | 68364100 | 63253200 | 62359966 |
| Slovakia | 150 | 0 (2) 54430861 | 0 (2) 59982000 | | Call embassy in Czech Republic (00420+) | Call embassy in Germany (0049+) |

| Country | Emergency phone number | US Embassies | UK Embassies | Australian Embassies | Canadian Embassies | New Zealand Embassies |
|---|---|---|---|---|---|---|
| Slovenia | 112 | 0 (1) 2005500 | 0 (1) 2003910 | 0 (1) 4254252 | Call embassy in Hungary (0036+) | 0 (1) 580 3055 |
| Solomon Islands | | | 21705 or 21706 | 21561 | Call embassy in Australia (0061+) | 21502 or 21503 |
| Somalia | | | Call embassy in Ethiopia (00251+) | | Call embassy in Kenya (00254+) | |
| South Africa | 10177 | 0 (12) 4314000 | 0 (12) 4217500 | 0 (12) 3423781 | 0 (12) 4223000 | 0 (12) 3428656 |
| Spain | 112/061 | (91) 5872240 | (91) 7008200 | (91) 3536600 | (91) 4233250 | (91) 5230226 |
| Sri Lanka | 1691095 or 1699935 | 0 (1) 448007 | 0 (1) 2437336 | 0 (1)2698767 | 0 (1) 5226232 | 0 (1) 2556701 |
| Sudan | | 0 (18) 3774701 | 0 (11) 777105 | | 0 (11) 790320 or 790322 | |
| Surinam | | 472900 | 402558 | | Call embassy in Guyana (00592+) | |
| Swaziland | 10177 | Call embassy in South Africa (0027+) | 4042581 | Call embassy in South Africa (0027+) | Call embassy in South Africa (0027+) | Call embassy in South Africa (0027+) |
| Sweden | 112 | 0 (8) 7835300 | 0 (8) 6713000 | 0 (8) 6132900 | 0 (8) 4533012 | 0 (8) 5063200 |
| Switzerland | 144 | 0 (31) 3577011 | 0 (31) 3597700 | 0 (22) 7999100 | 0 (31) 3573200 | 0 (22) 9290350 |
| Syria | 112 | 0 (11) 3331342 | 0 (11) 3739241 | Call Canadian embassy | 0 (11) 6116692 | |
| Taiwan | 110 | (2) 21622000 extn 2306 | (2) 21927000 | (2) 87254100 | (2) 25443000 | |
| Tajikistan | | 8 (372) 210348 | 8 (372) 242221 | | Call embassy in Kazakhstan (007+) | |

213

APPENDICES • Emergency numbers

| Country | Emergency phone number | US Embassies | UK Embassies | Australian Embassies | Canadian Embassies | New Zealand Embassies |
|---|---|---|---|---|---|---|
| Tanzania | 112 / 999 | 0 (22) 2668001 | 0 (22) 2110101 | Call Canadian embassy | 0 (22) 2112831 | See embassy in South Africa (0027+) |
| Thailand | 191 | 0 (2) 2054000 | 0 (2) 3058333 | 0 (2) 2872680 | 0 (2) 6360540 | 0 (2) 2542530 |
| Togo | 101 | 2212991 | See embassy in Ghana (00233+) | | 2213299 | |
| Tonga | | | 24285 or 24395 | 23244 | | 23122 |
| Trinidad and Tobago | 999 | 6225979 | 6222748 | 6284732 | 6226232 | Call Canadian embassy |
| Tunisia | | 0 (7) 1107000 | 0 (7) 1108700 | Call Canadian embassy | 0 (7) 1104000 | |
| Turkey | 155 | 0 (312) 4555555 | 0 (312) 4553344 | 0 (312) 4599500 | 0 (312) 4599200 | 0 (312) 4679054/6/8 |
| Turkmenistan | 03 | (12) 350045 | (12) 363462/3/4/6 | | Call embassy in Turkey (81090+) | Call embassy in Russia (8107+) |
| Tuvalu | | | Call embassy in Fiji (00 679+) | | | Call embassy in Fiji (00 679+) |
| Uganda | 999 | 0 (41) 259791 | 0 (31) 312000 | | 0 (41) 258141 | |
| Ukraine | 02 | 8 (44) 2469750 | 8 (44) 4903660 | 8 (44) 2357586 | 8 (44) 4641144 | Call embassy in Russia (8107+) |
| United Arab Emirates | 998/999 | 0 (2) 4142200 | 0 (2) 6101100 | 0 (2) 6346100 | 0 (2) 4071300 | 0 (4) 3317500 |
| United Kingdom | 112 | 0 (20) 74999000 | | 0(20) 73794334 | 0(20) 72586600 | 0(20) 79308422 |
| United States | 911 | | 1 (202) 5886500 | 1 (202) 7973000 | 1 (202) 6821740 | 1 (202) 3284800 |

214

| Country | Emergency phone number | US Embassies | UK Embassies | Australian Embassies | Canadian Embassies | New Zealand Embassies |
|---------|------------------------|--------------|--------------|---------------------|-------------------|----------------------|
| Uruguay | 999/911 | 0 (2) 4087777 | 0 (2) 6223630 | 0 (2) 9010743 | 0 (2) 9022030 | 0 (2/506221543) |
| Uzbekistan | 03 | 8 (71) 1205450 | 8 (71) 1206451 or 1207852/3/4 | | 8 (71) 1348385 | Call embassy in Russia (8107+) |
| Vanuatu | | | 23100 | 22777 | | 22933 |
| Venezuela | 171 | 0 (212) 9756411 | 0 (212) 2638411 | | 0 (212) 6003000 | Call embassy in Mexico (0052+) |
| Vietnam | 13 | 0 (4) 8431500 | 0 (4) 9360500 | 0 (4) 8317755 | 0 (4) 7345000 | 0 (4) 8241481 |
| Yemen | | 0 (1) 303155 | 0 (1) 264081/2/3/4 | | 0 (1) 208814 | |
| Yugoslavia | | See Serbia and Montenegro | See Serbia and Montenegro | See Serbia and Montenegro | See Serbia and Montenegro | See Serbia and Montenegro |
| Zambia | 999 | 0 (1) 250955 | 0 (1) 251133 | 0 (1) 253661 | 0 (1) 250833 | Call embassy in South Africa (0027+) |
| Zimbabwe | 995/999 | 0 (4) 250593 | 0 (4) 772990 or 0 (4) 774700 | 0 (4) 253661 | 0 (4) 252181/5 | Call embassy in South Africa (0027+) |

# 10: Basic phrases

### Help!
**Arabic:** Saa'idni!
**French:** Au secours!
**Hindi:** Bachao!
**Russian:** Pamageetyeh!
**Spanish:** ¡Socorro!
**Swahili:** Saidia!

### I need...a doctor/water/food/a phone
**Arabic:** Ahtaaj...tabeeb/maa'/akul/haatif
**French:** J'ai besoin...d'un docteur/de l'eau/de la nourriture/d'un téléphone
**Hindi:** Mujhe...daktar/pani/khana/teliphon...chahiye
**Russian:** Mnye nuzhen...vrach/vady/yedy/telefon
**Spanish:** Necesito...médico/agua/comida/teléfono
**Swahili:** Nahitaji... daktari/maji/chakula/simu

### I am...lost/sick/wounded
**Arabic:** Ana...dha'at/mariith/majrooh
**French:** Je suis...perdu/malade/blessé
**Hindi:** Main...gum gaya/bimar/ghayal...hoon
**Russian:** Ya zabloodilsya/ya zabolel/ya ranen
**Spanish:** Estoy...perdido/enfermo/herido
**Swahili:** Nimepotea/Nimegonjwa/Nimeumia

### I cannot find my companion
**Arabic:** La ajid sadiiqi
**French:** Je ne peux pas trouver mon compagnon
**Hindi:** Mujhe ... mera saathi nahin...mil raha
**Russian:** Ya ishchu svoego tovarishcha
**Spanish:** No puedo encontrar a mi compañero
**Swahili:** Rafiki yangu amepotea

### Airport/embassy...please hurry

**Arabic:** Mataar/safaara...bi suura' law samaht
**French:** Aéroport/ambassade...dépêchez-vous s'il vous plaît
**Hindi:** Hawai adda/dutavas... mujhe jaldi hai
**Russian:** Ayeraport/pasolstva... bweestra, pazhaaloosta
**Spanish:** Aeropuerto/embajada ... de prisa por favor
**Swahili:** Uwanja wa ndege/Ubalozi...nina haraka

### Sorry

**Arabic:** Ana asif
**French:** Désolé
**Hindi:** Maaf kijiye
**Russian:** Izvineetye
**Spanish:** Lo siento
**Swahili:** Samahani

### No offence was intended

**Arabic:** Ana atamana an ma ta'abtak
**French:** Aucune offense était voulue
**Hindi:** Maaf kijiye
**Russian:** Prosteetyeh
**Spanish:** No quería offender a nadie
**Swahili:** Hapana mabaya hapa

### Please accept this gift

**Arabic:** Tafudhal, xud haadha hadiiya
**French:** Veuillez accepter ce cadeau
**Hindi:** Meherbani karke yeh tohfa kabool kijiye
**Russian:** Primeetye, pazhaaloosta, etot skromnee padarok
**Spanish:** Acepte este regalo por favor
**Swahili:** Karibu, upokea zawadi hili

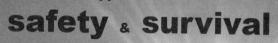

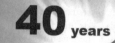

## Rough Guide credits

**Text editor:** Sally Schafer
**Design & layout:** Diana Jarvis
**Illustrator:** Murray Wallace

**Cartography:** Maxine Repath
**Proofreader:** Carole Mansur
**Production:** Julia Bovis

## Publishing information

This 1st edition published November 2005 by
**Rough Guides Ltd,**
80 Strand, London WC2R 0RL
345 Hudson St, 4th Floor,
New York, NY 10014, USA
14 Local Shopping Centre, Panchsheel Park,
New Delhi 110017, India
**Distributed by the Penguin Group**
Penguin Books Ltd,
80 Strand, London WC2R 0RL
Penguin Putnam, Inc.
375 Hudson Street, NY 10014, USA
Penguin Group (Australia)
250 Camberwell Road, Camberwell
Victoria 3124, Australia
Penguin Books Canada Ltd,
10 Alcorn Avenue, Toronto, Ontario,
Canada M4V 1E4
Penguin Group (New Zealand)
Cnr Rosedale and Airborne Roads
Albany, Auckland, New Zealand
Typeset in DIN, Garamond and Helvetica to
an original design by Diana Jarvis.

Printed in Italy by LegoPrint S.p.A

224pp includes index

A catalogue record for this book is available
from the British Library

ISBN 1-84353-406-1

The publishers and authors have done their
best to ensure the accuracy and currency of
all the information in **The Rough Guide to
Travel Survival**, however, they can accept
no responsibility for any loss, injury, or
inconvenience sustained by any traveller as
a result of information or advice contained
in the guide.

1   3   5   7   9   8   6   4   2

All travellers' tales are reproduced with
permission.

## Help us update

We've gone to a lot of effort to ensure that
the first edition of **The Rough Guide to
Travel Survival** is accurate. Our experts will
be the first to admit that survival is not an
exact science. There are different ways to
do things and if you spot anything from a
typo to a problem with the text or feel there's
important information left out that would
make the book better, we'd like to know.
We'll credit all contributions, and send a copy
of the next edition (or any Rough Guide if
you prefer) for the best letters. Everyone who
writes to us and isn't already a subscriber
will receive a copy of our full-colour, thrice-
yearly newsletter. Please mark letters **"Rough
Guide Travel Survival update"** and send to:
Rough Guides, 80 Strand, London WC2R
0RL, or Rough Guides, 4th Floor, 345 Hudson
St, New York, NY 10014. Or send an email to
**mail@roughguides.com**
  Have your questions answered and tell
others about your trip at
**www.roughguides.atinfopop.com**

# Acknowledgements

**The author**: First, I want to thank the survival and medical experts who served as the primary consultants for this book (listed alphabetically): Josh Bernstein, Alistair Cole, Laurence Gonzales, Brian Horner, David E. Johnson, Mors Kochanski, Cody Lundin, Charlie McGrath, Bill McGuire, Robert Young Pelton, Jeff Randall and Paul Rees. You might say this is the Dream Team of the survival world. Please check out their biographies at the end of the chapters, buy their books and take their survival courses.

Some of the specific topics were outside the expertise of this panel, and in such cases, those with even more specialized knowledge were consulted. The book would have had several noticeable holes without their help. Thanks to: Tim Baker, Joe Charleson, Kevin Frey, Richard Kithil Jr, Adriaan Louw, Doug Ritter and Peter Silvester. Each are among the world's best in their given fields.

I also want to thank the survivors who contributed their inspiring stories to this book (Tami Oldham Ashcraft, Peter DeLeo, Yossi Ghinsberg, Bruce Nelson and Mauro Prosperi). As if surviving their ordeal weren't effort enough, they had to think back through the painful details of the traumatic event yet again for the interview. Speaking and corresponding with them was a privilege – I'd be happy if I had a fifth of their courage and perseverance.

There were several others who helped get this book from an email proposal to a wad of dead tree with its own bar code. The first to have a crack at it was my agent, Michael Bourret (pronounced "Ber-RET," not "Boo-RAY"), who magically converted the emails into a contract. Also deserving thanks for this part of the process was Martin Dunford, the kind and insightful Rough Guides publisher who is not easily impressed by flattery, but saw fit to take on the project anyway. Sally Schafer was charged with editing the book from start to finish. If you open it to any page, read a little and find that you understand what you're reading, you have Sally to thank for it. Also responsible for this aspect is Kate Berens, the supervising editor, who would step in from time to time to help make sure things were going smoothly and that Sally and I were not playing solitaire. Murray joined the team a few months in, and quickly turned the book's descriptions into colourful illustrations that are even easier to follow than Ikea instructions. Allana Heames helped research the emergency embassy numbers when my eyes began to melt from prolonged computer monitor exposure. Mike Symons, Richard Trillo, Kevin Fitzgerald, Demelza Dallow, Geoff Colquitt, Megan Kennedy and Katherine Ball also had a hand in helping the book find its way to bookshelves. Thank you all.

**The editor**: Thanks to Jason Benham, Ruth Blackmore, Chris Field, Robert Gordon, Catherine Phillips, Richard Trillo and Clifton Wilkinson for putting together the Basic phrases section, Edward Aves for his words of wisdom, Kate Berens for her invaluable help and support during the editing process, Murray Wallace for his fantastic illustrations and patience, Diana Jarvis for her excellent design skills and dedication and Doug for his hard work and enthusiasm.

## Photo credits

Main front: Footprints in the desert © Strauss/Curtis/CORBIS
Back top: Loading a bus, Huehuetenango, Guatemala © Pep Roig/Alamy
Back bottom: Climber in Nepal © S. P. Gillette/CORBIS
Spine: Diver and shark © Firefly Productions/CORBIS

All illustrations by Murray Wallace © Rough Guides

# Index

Map entries are in colour